THE
Lazy
Realtor

Kick Back and Relax...
Your Guide To Building a Real Estate Sales
Machine That Rocks in Any Economy

WADE WEBB

Contents

Preface

Only those who will risk going too far
can possibly find out how far one can go.

T.S. Elliot

There is a saying, "Let it come from the horse's mouth." The story goes that, at a prestigious horse race, the owner of a horse said "my horse will win." The horse's trainer was also convinced that the horse would win and so was the jockey; but the horse said "no," and that was it. Ultimately, what counts is what comes from the horse's mouth.

This e-Book was not written by an expert sitting behind a desk. You too are going to hear it from the horse's mouth. The words on these pages come from a successful realtor's mouth, straight to you. They are a collection of actionable points, a guide to all of the methods and techniques, insider's tips and tricks you need to master, in order to achieve success as a Real Estate Agent.

The idea behind this book is that anyone can be successful, and it has a very simple, yet powerful, motto: "Successful people are no different, but they *do things differently.*" That is the whole concept, in a nutshell. Success is at arm's length. I made it, and you can make it too.

Zig Ziglar once said, "You can have everything in life you want, if you will just help enough other people get what they want." I believe that sharing my gift and motivating people to achieve success in sales can be as enriching for me as it will be for you.

In spite of relaxing in the comfort of the lifelong financial security awarded by my Real Estate business, I have devoted time and energy to writing this book because I am confident that reading it will be tremendously beneficial for your career.

Your success will, ultimately, be my success too. This is important to me because, unlike many experts who are putting out books every day, I was once in your shoes.

Remember; always hear it from the horse's mouth. The rest is worthless blabber.

My Story

It was the summer of 1992, and I was in my senior year of a Music and Education College degree. One day, casually browsing through the local newspaper, I came across an eye-catching ad in the "help wanted" section. It said "Students could earn $7,000 - $10,000 in one summer." Though it sounded too good to be true, the prospect got hold of me like a carrot being dangled in front of a horse. With little money and lots of time on my hands, I decided to respond and got myself an interview.

I remember finding the one blazer and tie I owned, putting them both on and heading downtown for the meeting, full of excitement and expectation. At the time, I knew nothing about sales; it was all completely alien to me. To my surprise, I was offered a job right on the spot. Over the following two weeks, I was trained to memorize a script for a two-and-a-half hour presentation created to sell encyclopedias.

Our sales team role played, recorded presentations, played them back again and memorized them, in order to prepare for selling encyclopedias door-to-door. I assumed we would be staying close to home, but I was wrong. The plan was for five university students to climb into one car and drive for 18 hours across three provinces, past the prairie province of Saskatchewan, into farm country, in the middle of nowhere. Looking back, I think I was pretty brave to do it, as I had just read "Death of a Salesman" in school, and I had no plans to become the new Willy Loman.

Each day in these small farming communities, we would drive out to local neighborhoods and scope out our sales territory, in order to get a feel for the area and figure out how we would tackle our long sales day. Every day at 3pm, we would be dropped off at our designated area. We were not allowed to return to the pick-up site until 10pm in the evening. Wearing t-shirts, shorts, and backpacks full of presentation materials, we headed out and knocked on between 250 and 350 doors in one day.

You may be wondering how we put up with the hard work. The fact is that it was all done in the understanding that we were on a mission from God, against illiteracy, to sell a set of encyclopedias and books, for $1999.99, to families that cared about their children's education.

After that experience of knocking on several doors per day, for many months on the road, selling lots of books, and earning thousands of dollars; I knew I had found my calling: it was in sales. In a slightly ironic turn of events, the lessons I learned back then, from potential clients telling me off over and over again, were invaluable, and they planted the seeds for my future; where the soil was as fertile as they get.

I still remember some of the lessons today, "Always be persistent. Never give up no matter what." One very important thing I learned was that the worst thing that could happen to me was the possibility of customers saying, "no," "no, thank you," or "get off my property." Looking back, that doesn't seem much different from what people are facing in Real Estate or any other direct sales field today. I figured that if that was the most terrible thing that could happen, it wasn't anything I couldn't deal with, so I just moved on.

Another thing I realized was that staying positive is the key to solving all problems. A few of my encyclopedia-selling colleagues were utterly miserable, and they made no money. I, myself, on the other hand, embraced the challenge with a smile, and made tons. In my travelling encyclopedia-boy days, I also learned something crucial: you need to know who you are as a sales person. You have to believe in yourself and your product. The truth is that you are no one if no one is buying from you.

With all that experience and knowledge behind my back, I called my father from a phone booth at a small farm town. I told him I was interested in getting into the Real Estate business. Full of excitement, I opened up to him and told him that sales were what I loved and what I felt to be my calling. I vividly remember the other end of the line being dead silent. I said to myself, "I am not going to be a high school band teacher; I am going to get into the Real Estate sales business."

At first, my dad said, "Don't be ridiculous." He then reminded me of all the practicing I had done and the money that had been spent on schooling for my Music degree. He thought that I was making a big mistake. Later, I did what any young person with a dream would have done; I completely ignored everything my father had said and proceeded to get my Real Estate license, plunging head on into the business.

Through selling encyclopedias door-to-door, I learned that a key to success in Real Estate, and in life, is to <u>always persevere</u>. Once you have that idea in your mind, the worst thing that can happen is someone rejecting your service and saying "no." The way to deal with that rejection is by understanding that it is aimed at whatever you are offering, rather than personally at you. <u>Avoid taking rejection personally</u>, as this can be the downfall of many a well-meaning rookie salesman.

These may seem like two very simple lessons, but, quite frankly, they changed my life.

1

Know Your Numbers

Budgeting

Sowing on the good soil

Financial success and success in business are all about sowing seeds on the good soil. If we want to know where the good soil is, before we get started in Real Estate, it is important to know our numbers. I have noticed that many seasoned salespeople have no grasp of their personal finances, or the numbers of the sales business.

How much would you and your sales career benefit, if you took the time to find out exactly how much your personal expenses cost you, each and every month? What would it mean to you and your business in Real Estate sales, if you knew exactly what your

> *"the sower went forth to sow; and as he sowed, some [seeds] fell by the way side, and the birds came and devoured them: and others fell upon the rocky places, where they had not much earth: and straightway they sprang up, because they had no deepness of earth: and when the sun was risen, they were scorched; and because they had no root, they withered away. And others fell upon the thorns; and the thorns grew up and choked them: and others fell upon the good ground, and yielded fruit, some a hundredfold, some sixty, some thirty."*
>
> *Matthew 13:3-9*

business` break-even figure is from a financial point of view? How many of us have taken the time to research and analyze what it costs us to function, at a minimum survival level, both personally and in business?

I would encourage you to start by developing your personal budget and then moving on to your business budget.

You will need to look at:

- **FIXED MONTHLY PERSONAL EXPENSES**

- **FIXED MONTHLY BUSINESS EXPENSES**

- **FIXED MONTHLY PERSONAL+BUSINESS EXPENSES**

Once you are fully aware of these NUMBERS, you will know how much you need to produce, in order to create a profit. That is, after all, why we are in this or any other type of business; to make a profit.

The Secret: Stop running after bills

Taking the time to work out budgets and to be aware of your expenses is important. One of the keys to my career success was for me to know exactly what my personal and business expenses were each month. Every month, I would write myself a check for those expenses and pay them, thus eliminating them right at the beginning.

Paying my personal and business costs in advance allowed me to focus on my business. After that was covered, I could concentrate on being the best salesperson I could be, and on my production, rather than on lingering expenses and wondering how and where those expenses were going to be covered.

I can't emphasize enough what it does to your self-esteem and to your personal life when, at the beginning of every month, both your personal and business expenses are met. This frees you up to do what you do best; helping people buy and sell Real Estate.

Put yourself first

Another success strategy I developed was to pay myself the same amount of money at the beginning of each month. For years in my career, I would just write myself a check for after-tax dollars corresponding to the same amount of money, month after month. For several years, I would still pay myself and live on that same amount of money. Then, at the end of the year, if I had had a better than normal production, I would have a surplus. It was this surplus that allowed me to invest, pay taxes, buy assets, buy real estate, and increase my personal net worth.

Banks, parents; just keep it safe...

You have to imagine that I was 21 years of age, when I started in the Real Estate industry. Back then, the idea of making a six figure income in Real Estate was completely foreign to me. I had never made more money than a regular restaurant waiter or an encyclopedia salesman. I quickly realized that I had no control over my new found earnings and I needed to put an accountability mechanism in place.

Certain prosperity and wealth advisors suggest you should have separate bank accounts at different banks; separate accounts for business, chequing, and savings. My idea was much simpler: I just gave all my earnings to my parents. You are going to laugh at this, but I am humbled to say that I had to ask my parents, for the first 8 years of my Real Estate career and then my office manager for the next 5 years, for my own money to spend. At the time, I didn't realize that the simple accountability system I had devised would, over the next 13 years, build me a fortune.

Therefore, do take the time to create business and personal budgets and know exactly what those numbers are. Know exactly what your minimum survival budget for each month is going to be. Then, you need to understand the concept of paying yourself first every month. But, more importantly, write yourself checks for your business and personal expenses at the start of the month, which will allow you to focus on your business. This will give you the necessary confidence, self-worth, and clarity to be strong, focused sales professional. Not to mention that, over a period of time, it will also help build your net worth.

> Financial prosperity has a universally accepted principle: it is critical to pay yourself first, before you pay your other bills, so that you can think of yourself as a creditor.
>
> The lesson behind this financial wisdom is that, if you wait to put money into savings until everyone else is paid, there will be nothing left for you. The result is that you will keep postponing your savings plan until it's too late to do anything about it.

Buyer & Seller Cycles

Your next strategy should be to understand the cycles of Real Estate; namely, the math of production and what we want to produce. There are two distinct cycles in Real Estate. The first cycle is the buying cycle of property and the second cycle is the selling cycle of Real Estate.

Seller cycle

You begin by prospecting and looking for the seller. Once you have found the seller, you present your sales proposal to them and list their property for sale. The marketing begins next, when you attract interested buyers to write offers. With due negotiations, the sale is clinched to the satisfaction of both the seller and the purchaser. After the sale, those sellers become your satisfied clients.

Buyer cycle

The cycle with buyers is similar: you find the buyer and ensure that the buyer is financially qualified and specifically ascertain their needs. You must show the buyer different choices of property that suit their needs and wants, write up offers, negotiate with the seller, and finalize the sales deal. Once the transaction is over, the buyer is a satisfied client.

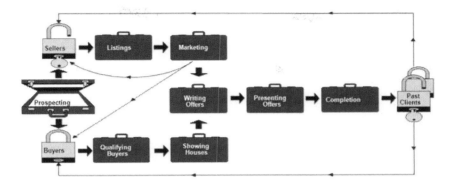

You should understand the basic difference between these two cycles.Top producing agents focus on the seller cycle, rather than on the buyer cycle. You know why? **The seller cycle is more profitable and it has a higher return on your time investment** compared to the hours spent with a buyer.

Numbers that rule your world

Think about this:

The National Association Of Realtors® (NAR) has obtained proven statistics that, on average, **the amount of hours invested in business related activities for a buyer is approximately 32 hours, whereas it is just 8 hours in the case of sellers for the same amount of money earned.** Which one would you rather focus your activities on? The seller, of course!

This explains why **top producers in the Real Estate business are top "listers".** They have tons of inventory and tons of listings. They also create lots of spin-off business.

The cycle is different with the seller than with the buyer on the marketing stage. Here, you are able to market to other prospective buyers and prospective sellers and spin off the marketing of the same listing. In fact, NAR also estimates that an average listing can spin off approximately 15 pieces of business, consisting of other listings or sales.

The power of spinning

Listings can generate those buyers and sellers, but you also have an opportunity with each listing to double end, or collect two ends of the commissions, when both the buyer and the seller are your clients. This way, you make more money in a shorter space of time. In their turn, buyers basically bring in a single-client transaction, but they could become repeat customers or they could refer you and give you more business.

The key ingredient to the cycle is to understand the power of double ending and **the power of spinning off and getting 15 more transactions from every single listing.** Another ingredient known by top producers is the understanding that selling property requires lots of skills: presentation, questioning, dialog, rapport building, marketing, negotiation, price reduction, and closing the sale efficiently and effectively. Not all of these skills come naturally, but they are practiced and learned over time.

You must understand the power of budgeting and being in business from a position of profitability. Never underestimate the power of paying yourself first and being able to focus on buying and selling Real Estate. Know the power of the Real Estate cycle, when working with a buyer (as opposed to a seller) and the opportunities that lay in front of you. This is a valuable lesson to ensure that your Real Estate business is an intelligent mechanism, where the leads continue to come in from the marketing of your own inventory.

Statistics

The magic numbers

When it comes to numbers, statistics are the key. The most important statistics for you are the **list-to-sales ratios. Investigate** and know what the average listing is selling for, percentage-wise, versus the asking price. Find that information for all product types and know what percentage from their asking price the seller can, realistically, expect to get. For example, in our particular marketing area, the average seller is expecting 92% of their asking price. This means that sellers are usually getting an average 8% discount from the asking price.

Another important statistic you need to be aware of is the **amount of inventory available** for each product type listed for sale, but lying unsold. The number of pieces of property available contrasted with the number of sold items can help you identify the market's consumption rates and inventory trends.

The homes listed on the market which haven't been sold are called expired areas. Knowing expired areas well is good, in order to learn what the chances are, and how many listings you need (percentage-wise), to actually sell. For example, in our local market, our expired ratio is about 36%, meaning that only one in three homes listed is selling. The remaining two out of three are coming off the market without being sold each year.

Keeping it real

Why is it important to know the list-to-sell percentage? When sellers are listing their homes, they are expecting to get their asking price. If you don't know your statistics, you cannot advise sellers listing with you, as to how much they can expect to get from their asking price. The sellers will then also know that, if they get anything over 92% of their asking price, you are doing a great job.

You also need to present a realistic picture to your sellers. They need to know that two out of three homes are not selling, in the context of current market trends. This will mentally prepare them to accept the fact that they have only a 33% chance of selling. They should be honestly told, in clear terms, that, in order to sell, their asking price should be competitive in relation to the prices of similar listings in their area.

Listing cycles

It is also useful to know for **how many days a listing remains on the market** and how long it is taking for all product types and each individual product type to sell. A lot of sellers assume that this only takes 30 days or a couple of weeks since the listing are first on the market. In our local market, we are selling residential products in approximately 92 days, on average. This is the time the property is active, until it becomes unconditional or subject-free[1].

But it can be even more practical to finalize the transaction and get the seller their proceeds. Normally, another 50% of the time, that is 46 days, is to be added to cover this. For example, this is the time from unconditional subject removals[2] until completion[3] or closing day. Again, **educating your sellers and buyers about the practicalities of the business** is always best. Do not over-promise or under-deliver, as this will not help you succeed in your business.

The right price

The other final and most important statistics you need to know are your average property selling prices and the median[4] prices in your local markets. **Know where the fish are biting**; where the inventory and the price point is. What are those numbers and where is the activity? **What percentage of activity is selling below the average price and above the average price?** You need to be able to answer all these questions with precision.

---

[1]   A subject-free offer is a proposal from the buyer where the buyer cannot walk away if the seller accepts.

[2]   This is the moment when the buyer agrees to pay the agreed price on the completion date, unconditionally.

[3]   This is the finalization of the transaction; when the buyer pays and becomes the legal owner of the property.

[4]   The median is an indicator of central tendencies. It is a mathematic variable which differs from the average, and is more representative of market tendencies and frequency.

The activity zone

There is nothing worse than working in a market niche where there is no activity at all, or in an area so far above the average price or the median price that no one is buying or selling. If you are aware of how the average and median price points change every month, you will be in a better position to cope with the market's ups and downs.

Pricing psychology

At the end of the day, it is the list-to-sell ratio that sellers can expect to get, and not their asking price. It is also useful to understand that **buyers need to be educated about the sellers' mentality of coming down only about 8%** of their asking price. Therefore, if you get anything over and above an 8%, you have done a great job for the buyer, and buyers need to understand this.

Essentially, both buyers and sellers need to know that the whole process does take time. This factor influences how long you will sign up a listing for. In the market described here, you would need to take a listing for a minimum of 6 months, in order to cover the entire time the process takes. **Knowledge of monthly market statistics** allows you, as a Real Estate professional, to see market trends and opportunities, which may escape other agents, buyers, and sellers. This is valuable information which will increase your professional expertise, as well as boost your reputation in your local market.

Take the time each month to internalize list-to-sell ratios, days-on-market, average and median prices, consumption and expiry rates, and really understand what is happening in the business. This profound knowledge of the Real Estate market will become a prime differentiating factor between you and the competition.

The people behind the numbers: the relationship business

It's not about you "The purpose driven life"
By Rick Warrens

The key to everything I have learned in almost two decades in the Real Estate business can be summed up in one word: relationships. **We are in the relationship business and our success is tantamount to our ability to create rewarding relationships.** Without successful relationship-building, all the prospecting methods, sales scripts, presentations, tips, and ideas presented in this book mean nothing. As it is the case with almost any other area of existence, the ability to create and maintain meaningful relationships will produce the greatest yields in your real estate profession.

As Rick Warrens wisely summed it up in the above quote, the secret to **your success will lie on the ability to focus on everyone else, instead of yourself.** This ability to focus on others at all times has become extremely elusive in our modern societies, where entitlement and quick self–gratification are the rule.

I am sometimes amazed by some of the incredibly successful people I have relationships with, both personally and professionally. The greatest lesson I have learned from them is this: just before we finish our time together, talking on the phone or just passing by, they always take the time to ask, "Is there anything I can do for you?" I am always blown away by the realization that these incredibly busy, successful, popular individuals would sincerely care to take the time to ask little old me. "Is there anything I can do for you today?" But then again, that is precisely the reason they are so successful: because they care, and they know how to show how much they care.

The four gifts

In his popular book "The Generosity Factor," Ken Blanchard said that we have four gifts we can give people, both in life and in business. These are:

TIME
TOUCH
TALENTS
TREASURES

Time is more precious than gold, water, and air. It is something that you cannot make more of; it is limited, and hence, it is also the most powerful gift you can give anybody. Society is so busy being busy, that we often don't have time to give to our clients. Sometimes, we close the sale and never see our clients again. What do you think it could do for your business, if you scheduled regular face to face time with your clients?

Most of the time, we don't even take the time to have family dinners. What ever happened to the regular weekly family dinners where everyone shared the gift of time? Times have changed, and it seems like we are running on a treadmill of life that keeps us from getting off. Who doesn't enjoy a pat on the back, a hug, someone shaking their hand and saying, "well done"? This is an inherent human quality; it is the greatest feeling just to be held or to be physically appreciated in some way.

Personally, I grew up in a family of people who didn't show their appreciation to each other through physical contact. Over the years, I have learned to work on this every day; on developing the ability to share the gift of physical touch with others. It is the greatest gift that I can give my loving wife and children, who would be happy with nothing else but physical touch from their husband and father.

Someone once told me that it wasn't the gift of touch that had the greatest impact on others, but depriving them of the opportunity to give us their greatest gift, namely, TOUCH. The key is to be open to both give and receive physical appreciation.

We have all been blessed with certain gifts that we have to share with the rest of the world. I myself have been blessed with a passion and talent for teaching, speaking, and mentoring. It is my purpose in life to use these gifts daily, to impact and improve other people's lives.

The greatest gift for me and my success in Real Estate sales has nothing to do with money. Don't get me wrong, I do care about money, but what really gives me a sense of fulfillment is to be in the position today to give it away; to use my wealth to help others and leave a legacy behind me.

Once a year, I set out to visit a third world country and invest not just my money but also my own physical time and work on a mission project overseas. That annual event impacts me greatly, filling me with purpose and energy. It represents the most rewarding time and financial investment of my life.

Think about this: what are some of the most affluent people in the world doing with all of their wealth and power? Bill Gates, Bono and Warren Buffet are all using their wealth and power to impact and improve the world because all the money in the world isn't enough in life, even for them.

Take the time to sit down and really listen to people, ask questions, become interested in others. Discover whether you like them or they like you. Are they people you could spend time with? Would they be willing to spend time with you? Do they possess an attractive personality? Can you picture yourself serving them with enthusiasm?

Feedback makes perfect

One of the best places to start in my business and to increase my relationships with clients is to always ask for feedback. How am I doing? What can I do differently? What can be done better? As Zig Ziglar put it, "People don't care what I know, until they know that I care." There is no better way to show them that you care than constantly asking for feedback. Take the time, as Brian Buffini always said and Big 3 your clients:

1. **How am I doing and what could we be doing better?**
2. **What can I do to help you personally or professionally?**
3. **I just want you to know that I appreciate you and the impact you have on me and my business.**

Feedback in practice

Once a year, I take the time to sit face to face with all my clients and have lunch with them in small groups, to ask them for their input regarding my business. Basically, I request their feedback on things like, what I can do better and give them an opportunity to make my successful business even more successful. During one of these lunches, one particular client told me that, over the years, they had never had anyone else that they were doing business with care to ask them for their input or even act like what they had to say was important. In other words, my clients couldn't believe that they had a chance to help run my business, because nobody else was giving them that chance.

Getting to know people

How well do you really know someone? What would it do to your business, if you knew details like someone's hobbies, favorite food, drink, restaurant, music, sports team, etc.? How about wedding anniversaries or home purchase anniversaries, birthdays and so on? Imagine what you could do with this important information. Knowing these things would give you multiple opportunities to build and extend those valuable relationships, which may become the key to both your personal life and your business.

Let me illustrate with a story: I remember one of my clients referred three connections to my business. All three referrals turned out to be excellent, profitable prospects. I really wanted to show my client how much I appreciated their business. So, I took the time to do a bit of research on him, in order to find a suitable way of thanking him. As a result of my efforts, I was able to set him and his wife up with a weekend at their favorite hotel, where their favorite restaurant was located. I had the manager of the hotel call him and his wife inviting them both to the hotel for a romantic getaway, which included dinner for two at the restaurant, spa packages and a full complimentary breakfast. A few days later, my client came into the office in shock: he couldn't believe that I knew what their favorite place to stay was! His wife had loved the spa, and they had both enjoyed the romantic time away from their two children. In fact, my client had completely forgotten that I had collected all of these details one day over coffee with him.

People love talking about themselves. **This kind of crucial information can be fairly easy to obtain and, as you can see, people will volunteer it and then forget all about it, giving you great opportunities to wow and dazzle them.** Of course, you don't need to offer every single one of your clients a complimentary getaway, but sometimes the smallest thing, like sending them a nice card on their anniversary, can mean the world to them and make a big difference to you, the relationship and ultimately your business.

Databases – Relationship Lists

Tell me who you know...

One summer I was vacationing in Florida, a local broker shared a story with me over dinner. It was about how every time he ordered at a drive thru he would ask the cashier what the person behind him was having and how much it cost. He would hand the cashier his business card with a note written on the card saying "Hope you have a great day." He would then pay for the other car's meal and ask the cashier to hand the strangers his card, together with their food. One day, he received a phone call from a man saying, "We have never met but a few months back you bought me lunch. I kept your card and never forgot. My sister has recently passed away and I would like you to come and list the oceanfront apartment block she owned." That one phone call made the broker enough commission for his entire year.

So, yes, it is all about numbers, and yet, **it is all about people.** Now, let's look at how numbers and people connect.

Potential clients everywhere

The most important people-numbers you need to be aware of are the number of people and the amount of times the average North American (or any geographical group) moves over a period of time.

Research shows that the average North American moves about every 3-5 years. If every North American is moving every 3-5 years, then you can anticipate that 20% of all North Americans are moving each year. Apply that general 20% to your own database (one out of every five people) and you know that there is a high chance that one out of five of them are going to be involved in Real Estate business this year.

What do I mean by this? For example, if you have 250 clients in your database and you use the 20% rule, you would have 50 of your clients or 50 people you know, who respect and trust you, move in the course of your calendar year of business. If you go on and do the math, that is 50 times the average commission in your area, this equates to a substantial amount of money, which would signify a fairly good year in Real Estate.

For example our average commission in our particular area is approximately $6,500 per transaction. If we finish 50 transactions, it is equal to more than $300,000 in gross commission earnings within one year of real estate. This is an excellent earning amount for most people.

Multiplying leads

One thing you need to understand is that one person in your database knows an average of 285 other people. So, it is important to understand that one person in your sphere has the ability to introduce you to another 285 people. Nice people tend to know other nice people. Difficult people tend to know other difficult people; as the saying goes, birds of a feather tend to flock together. Therefore, when you find somebody that you truly enjoy doing business with, to help them buy or sell property, you need to foster and nurture that relationship, understanding the power of those people, who may be able to introduce you to another 285 people just like them.

You should not underestimate the power of the 285 or the 20% rule. Think about what realtors spend in money, time, and effort getting their clients. Ironically, most of them don't spend any money, time, or resources in keeping their clients and tapping into this valuable source of business. The potential of tapping into the 20% and the other 285 great friendly people is thus lost. It is a pity we don't spend more time and effort on building relationships with people who can become advocates for you and your business.

Divide and conquer

I like to take my database of clients or, as I refer to it, "my relationships list," and categorize them according to the parameters that are most helpful to my relationship-building. **My first category is that of raving fans; these are your AAA+ clients.** They are the people who insist on dealing with you, will do business with you no matter what, and constantly refer you. They will, in fact, never consider doing anything with anybody else but you, and they do business with you on a regular basis. Now, this group of people will not be very large, but the more you work on increasing its number, the raving fan base of you and your business, the more successful and easier your business becomes.

The second category would be your clients, your sphere of influence; your friends and family, or people who know you, trust you, and would be glad to do business with you. The key to managing this category B clientele is that you need to foster your relationships with these people. You need to show them your competency and character, in order to build their trust, to the point where they will insist on doing business with you and nobody else. As your advocacy with this group grows, they too will introduce you to the 285 people that they are connected to. The key is to try and focus your time and energy on the B client-list category, trying to turn them into the raving fans of the AAA+ category.

The final category of C clients can be classed under the term "acquaintances". Acquaintances are people you may not know well. However, they do know you and appreciate you, and even trust you, but, for example, you do not exchange holiday cards with them, and you don't meet them very often. These acquaintances need to be granted the courtesy of being asked if they would mind being added to your database. One of the biggest faults I have seen is that people take private directories, lists of people that they don't have a relationship with and automatically send them things like mail, without permission. The right way to do it is to contact the people in this list and ask them if they would mind being added to your database.

Expanding your database

Learn to either purge your acquaintance group by either phoning or visiting them. Ask them if they have a Real Estate agent they know, like, and trust and would refer people to. If case they don't, could that be you? You could then mention how your database is updated from time to time and you send out valuable information to your database list. Would they be interested in receiving that sort of information? If they agree, then you can start building a relationship with them to the point where you can add them to your B category. If they disagree, then you simply remove them from your list.

Turning strangers into cheerleaders

So, let us review the categories in your database. The AAA+'s your raving fans and cheerleading teams. Your relationship with them is something you should maintain at all costs, because they will be the best advocates for your business. Then, there is your B group of prospective clients who will only really give business to you if you ask them for it. It is your responsibility to work on these relationships, to build that trust and ask those people for those referrals. This way, you can tap into the extra 285 people each one of them knows.

The C category is made up of people you are acquainted with. These are people you need to ask permission from, in order to add them to you database and send them regular information. If they agree, they move into the B group and if they don't, they are a D and you just delete them. If you are not sure if a person is a C, then do the holiday card test; ask yourself whether you would send them one or not. That always works.

Just out of curiosity...

One of my favorite lines is, "just out of curiosity; do you have a Real Estate professional you use, like your doctor, lawyer or accountant, somebody that you receive valuable information and advice from about your Real Estate opportunities on a regular basis? If not, I would like to be that person. From time to time I send out valuable information regarding local markets, financing tips, home renovation ideas, and much more. Would that be of interest to you? Where is the best place I can send this to?"

While sending out unwanted information to people who don't know you may be a total waste, something like the speech above will always yield a fair number of positive results.

Lead Generation

Glengarry style

The last set of statistics that I find important is the ones that have to do with prospecting. **Prospecting is simply a number game.** Statistics teach us many things. First of all, you need to know what the **average commission** end is in your area. Know what the **average list side or sell side** is, so that you can calculate how many transactions you need each month, in order to cover your expenses and business costs, plus make a profit each month. For example the average commission end is $6,500 in our market area.

Then, **focus on your target number of transactions.** In my business, I was not satisfied unless I was doing a minimum of 7 transactions a month, which was giving me the profitability I was looking for, as well as covering personal and business expenses every month. Your number will be different, of course, but you need to take the time to calculate it.

Cashing in on leads

Lead generation statistics tell us that, **for every 100 people they come across, the average salesperson closes for a sit down or an appointment with 10 of them.** Whether they are seller-listing appointments or buyer appointments, the average agent should be focusing on getting a contract (either a buyer contract or a seller contract) from at least three out of those ten appointments. Statistics also show that you can expect to get paid on 2 out of 3 of those contracts, in a balanced market[5].

How many people do you need to talk to this year,
to reach the number of contracts you require?

For example, if you were looking at thirty final contracts this year, you need 100 appointments to get those thirty contracts, which means that you need to prospect and talk to 1000 people this year.

Control your workday, control your income

Anticipate the number of the days you will be working each year and calculate how many contacts you will need to be talking to each day. For instance, if you need three sales this month, then you will need to have nine contracts, meaning that you will need thirty listing or buyer appointments, which will require you to talk to 300 people in one month.

Just to summarize, we are in the relationship business. In Real Estate, we need to meet with people every day. Take the time to know:

> How many DAYS you need to work?
>
> How many PEOPLE you need to contact each day?
>
> How many APPOINTMENTS you have to close?
>
> How many CONTRACTS you need signed each month?

That is how you will be able to fulfill your business, personal, and profit goals. This is your simple but powerful business plan for Real Estate success. There are so many agents who fail to plan and plan to fail in this business that only 20% of the agents do 80% of the business. You can be in that 20% today.

---

[5] Also Transitional Market refers to when there are 5-7 months of listing inventory available.

2

Sales and Power Prospecting

Enter the World Wide Web

The Internet has changed the Real Estate business by helping us avoid many hassles. Years ago agents had Multiple Listing Service or MLS for listing all the details of property, buyers, and sellers in catalogues, which were available at Real Estate offices. Clients had to commute all the way to the Agent's office, to get a copy of the MLS catalogue. Agents had to spare the time with every visiting prospect, even for a preliminary enquiry.

Today, a seller can contact and hire the agent directly online, after researching agents, market trends, and pricing. Similarly, a buyer can gather all the details of available pieces of property from the published MLS, select a suitable one, and then approach the agent online for further viewing and purchasing.

The power of connecting

After the rather impersonal first contact, comes the person to person connection. People rely on their relationship with a Real Estate professional, not just to provide a transaction, but to provide advice, interpretations, and education, so that they can come to an informed decision that fits all of their needs. Sales transactions come from relationships rather than just a strictly-business procedure.

This has led to a shift in how Real Estate professionals now interact with their clients. They have to move from a transactional sales situation to one where they need to be trusted. This can only come from a relational sales style. People will not buy from, sell through, or do business with agents they cannot trust.

If sales people are only focusing on one thing, they should be focusing on the relationship with the client, and the relationship begins with an appointment. At this instance, you and the client spend time to get to know one another. The days are gone when people were simply trying to close for the deal and the transaction; they now have to close to get a sit-down. Today's Real Estate sales pros need to close for an appointment, to sit down with either a buyer or a seller and answer the single question that both buyers and sellers are always asking: what's in it for them? This is not about the benefits of doing business with you; it is all about what's in it for the buyer and for the seller. That is the only question they want to ask.

What's in a sit-down

I have a friend who specializes in high-end homes and luxury Real Estate. One of the things he needs to do, in order to succeed in that niche market, is regularly attend fundraising, charity, and networking events. He once said to me, "I am just not the schmoozing kind of person. I didn't even know how to create small-talk with people at this type of events until I discovered the FORD technique."

F AMILY
O CCUPATION
R ECREATION
D REAMS

This technique allowed him to engage people quickly and keep them interested, as they developed a sense of comfort around him. The method begins by asking people about their **Family (F)**, and talking about them and their family for as long as you can. Then you ask them about both their current **Occupation (O)** and what kind of jobs they have done in the past.

He would then ask them about **Recreation (R)** and what they did for fun or as a hobby. Finally, he would ask them about their **Dreams (D)** and what their goals and aspirations for the future were.

This simple but powerful tool would allow him to **build instant trust, credibility, and comfort** in his rapport with people from any social level or business field. Remember: the Family, Occupation, Recreation, and Dreams technique will open the doors to any face to face situation, and it will make your sit-down appointments more successful than ever before!

By encouraging and mastering the dynamics of sit-down appointments, you are able to build trust and rapport, ask and answer questions, and learn about what the client wants. Sooner than later, your ability to close from such appointments will increase. As a result, once your ability to build a rapport with clients starts working better and faster, you will experience success in Real Estate sales.

Keep the leads coming

One of the benefits of sit-down appointments is steady lead generation. Set aside a few hours every day for meeting with people who want to buy or sell Real Estate. Now, you might wonder why lead generation is important. All the time, I see agents so focused on individual transactions and clients, that they pay little attention to prospecting.

What they do is this: they prospect a little and discover a buyer, and they work with that one buyer in finding them a suitable piece of property. But, while they are working with that one prospect or transaction, they are forgetting the importance of lead generation on a daily basis. Sooner or later, their activity drops to little or nothing, and they are back to square one. They have to start the whole process again; discovering one prospect from a stack of contacts, and so on.

Lead generation should always be done on a daily basis. It is really important for you to be bringing in more clients through the back door, while you are thanking your satisfied clients and showing them out the front door.

> Lead generation is like a Ferris wheel:
> You bring people on as you move people off

While you are bringing more people on, you are moving more people off, as their transactions complete. This is how your business grows and becomes consistent. It may sound simple, and, in a way, it is; but most people forget about it, and that is why their business remains stagnant.

It is vitally important for your success to have an ever-increasing lead generation process in place.

Many Real Estate agents often don't understand why, although they do the same sort of things over and over again, their business never grows. Consider someone like Tiger Woods. How much practice did he have to do when he first started on the golf course? How many times did he work on his swing or his follow-through to become the best player in the world? Now, how much time do agents spend practicing their sales craft?

Work on your swing

Real Estate is much the same as sports, except that, in our field, you are **practicing your presentations, your follow-through, your lead generation, and your closings.** You should do this to the point where you don't have to practice nearly as hard to get it right. Know your dialogs; develop your listening and communication skills. Learn how to steer conversations in the direction you want them to go, and get to the point where what you do successfully becomes second nature to you.

> **If you want to improve YOUR BUSINESS,
> you need to improve YOURSELF.**

Be constantly learning; that's the spirit.

In life and in business the success you have is related to the value you see in yourself. The late Jim Rohn[6] once said, "**Work harder on yourself than you do on your job.**"

In Real Estate, you sell yourself and an experience. Your persona and the Real Estate experience you create for people need to be memorable; something people will look back at with admiration and pleasure.

Prospecting

Business guru Harvey Mackay once told the story of something that happened to him in New York, to illustrate creativity in meeting customers' needs. When Mackay got into an NY cab one day, the driver presented him with a printed mission statement, which said he intended to get his passengers to their destination "safely, courteously, and on time." He offered Mackay an array of CDs to choose from and the use of his cell phone. When the cab came to a stop, the driver presented Mackay with a brown-bagged snack with his card inside. The taxi driver's innovative approach and pride in his business garnered him thousands of extra dollars in tips every year.

There are countless methods of prospecting and finding new leads and opportunities in Real Estate. Some of them are:

---

[6]   A world famous business philosopher.

PROSPECTING METHODS

✓ **Person To Person** (such as door-knocking)

✓ Kiosks, Social Events, Meetings, Networking

✓ By **Telephone**, Using a **Reverse Directory** or **Phoning People about Listings and Sales**

✓ **Following Up** via Telephone or by Mail

✓ **Direct Mail** using Personal Address Mail, Non-Addressed Bulk Mail, Ad-Mail, and Flyers

✓ **Online Campaigns**: Email Drip Campaigns, Websites, E-Newsletters, E-Flyers, Online Lead Generation

✓ **Response-Generated Marketing** using Toll-Free Phones for Reports And Tips, to Capture Leads

✓ Offline methods such as **Signs and Print Advertisements**

The important thing to remember with all of these methods is that you have to take the time to discover your inner sweet spot, or what you are good at. Keep in mind that consumers are looking for:

Honesty

Integrity

An Internet presence

A Good Website experience

A Good Email/Telephone experience

What is prospecting?

According to the Webster Dictionary, prospecting is "the act of digging or searching for something worthwhile." In fact, it is the term used in mining, when a mining company goes to an area where they believe there could be valuable minerals underground. They don't know that there is gold or diamonds there, but they still know that there is a fair chance for it, and they just dig on. In Real Estate, it is the prospects that want to buy or sell (preferably to sell, as you learned in step one) that are your gold.

Always remember that your main objective is not to close for that sale, or to close for that listing, but, instead, to **close for the sit-down and the appointment and to build that relationship.** You use those opportunities to develop trust and rapport with the prospect. And, don't forget, when you are having your sit-down, the most important single question your client wants answered is, **"What is in it for me?"**

Choosing your prospects

A bona-fide prospect is basically any person who wants to buy or sell property now or in the near future. When I say, "near future," I mean that **you want to be working with people who are looking to do something within a 30, 60 or 90-day timeline.** I am not saying you should ignore prospects that might be looking at doing something in terms of months (say up to 24 months). However, the latter would need to be kept in a separate part of your database, so you can keep in touch with them and send them valuable information on a regular basis. You may also use newsletters or email drips[7] so that, when these people are ready to do something, your name is the one they think of first.

---

[7]   Email drip marketing is a form of marketing that sends email messages to subscribers based on a schedule. Using special software, the emailing schedule is set to send emails at the sender's preferred interval.

The importance of WHEN

Now you can focus your time and energy on the prospects who want to buy or sell over the course of the next 30, 60, or 90 days. How do we determine the prospect and their timeline? All you need to remember is the most important qualifying question in Real Estate: when?

When do you need an answer to your question?

When do you need to move?

When do you need to be in your new home?

When do you need to sell?

All these *when* questions will help you establish a timeline for your prospect. Listen to the answers, but if the prospect has mentioned something in the 30, 60, or 90 day timeline, they are the ones you need to focus on right away. Make sure you keep the other ones in the database you have set up for future focus.

Getting started

I am always surprised when I hear Real Estate agents wondering why the people in their sphere of influence are not using them on a short-term basis, and why these people seem to be the worst sorts of prospects at the beginning of their career, but then turn into the best prospects, as their career becomes more successful.

The answer is this: If you had millions of dollars and you were investing in the stock market, and you knew of a broker you liked and trusted, but who had only six days of experience in the investment business; would you give that person those millions of dollars? Your answer would surely be, "no." That is why people in your own sphere of influence are more likely to wait and see how your career develops, before they start giving you their business; no matter how much they like and trust you.

Now, you don't only have to find and develop prospects who don't know how little experience you have, but you also have to take the time to **keep the other people in your sphere of influence**

regularly updated with listings and sales because, over time, you are planning to get their business too.

From I to We

What do you think will happen if you can keep your contacts informed of your successes with sales and listings? At first, you may have to start mentioning the successes of other agents in your office. Being honest of course, but you could say something like, "we just listed..." or "we just sold..." Their perception of you will change from a "we will see" to an "I like doing business with a successful person, and I know just the person."

It is important to note that the people in your sphere of influence are not going to worry so much about your personal success with sales and listings, if they see that the firm that you work for is being successful. They are not so concerned with the "I" as opposed to the "we," and so their perception of you will be improved.

Increase your chances of success and constantly demonstrate your competence in Real Estate within your own sphere of influence by keeping in touch with those people, letting them know about how well you are doing, and asking them whether or not there is anything you can do for them.

The irony is that, if you ask a new agent why he or she got into the business in the first place, the answer will often be, "because I like dealing with people." Paradoxically, though, very few agents like prospecting for clients. They are almost afraid of the whole process. This is where you need to remember that the worst thing a person could say to you is, "no, thank you" or "get off my property." If that is the worst thing you can expect when prospecting, and you are mentally prepared for it, you can surely cope with that. You also need to remember that, if you are rejected, <u>it is your service that is actually being rejected</u>, rather than you personally, or maybe they just don't need Real Estate advice <u>at that time.</u>

The two important parts of that last statement are, "it is your service," and "at that time." They might need your service later, so, you shouldn't forget that. If you come into a meeting with the expectation that people will be pleasant and nice to deal with, then 90% of the time they will be, especially if you are pleasant and nice to them. Believe that you have a valuable service to offer people. In James Allen's book, "As A Man Thinketh," he states that **what you think and what you believe is what you will become.**

I would encourage you to always have these thoughts:

> **Someone Does Need To Use Your Service**
>
> **Somebody Will List With You Today**
>
> **Someone Will Buy From You Today**

They just don't know it yet.

Be in the moment

One of the key factors about prospecting is that you need to stay really focused. Make sure you are *in the moment* and in tune with what you are doing.

One day, I was giving a conference and someone asked me at what times he should focus on prospecting. The answer to this question would be: if you are someone who does their best work at night, then work in the evening, if you are an early bird, then probably mornings, lunch-times and early afternoons are more suitable for you. There is never any time of day that is better than the other, but it should be <u>a time of day that works for you.</u>

Tracking success

Have your contacts systemized, have systems in place to track what you are doing, what your successes are and when they are occurring. Also, make a note of the number of calls you make in a day and how many people you talk to. Keep track of the type of successes you get from each and every call, contact, or activity. This will help you realize which times of the day work best for you. Later, you can schedule your appointments to take place at your most productive times of day.

Another question I often get asked is, "What is the method to use to talk to prospects or what should you prospect on?" The answer to that question is this: Ask yourself, "What do you believe you are good at? What prospecting methods do you enjoy? What prospecting methods would are you prepared to do for a few hours a day, on a regular basis?"

Do it your way

Your answers to these questions will represent the prospecting methods you should use the most. Don't worry about the type of methods that you won't enjoy, or that you don't believe you are good at, because you are not going to want to do those things on a regular basis.

In his book about personal strengths, Marcus Buckingham talks about how people in some organizations only do what they do best, with fantastic results; I absolutely share his point of view. You should not waste your energy on things that you are not good at, or which you do not consider to be your strengths or do not enjoy. Instead, focus on those things that you are passionate about, which you will do and can't wait to do. Imagine what your success ratio will be, if you just follow that simple rule!

Understand the importance of persistence. I loved the moments in my career when I received those magical phone calls when someone would say, "Hi, it's Mr. and Mrs. Seller. We have been receiving your emails [your newsletter] for quite some time. We were just talking the other night and we decided it was time for us to sell. We would like you to come over."

These calls came from persistence, from constant follow-up and regular contact with people.

> ## Don't focus on *Results*
> ## Focus on *Activity*

You don't measure your success by the results, but by the scope of your activities, believing that those activities will pay off.

Become an EXPERT

Finally, when prospecting, try to create a brand for yourself in a certain niche, to increase your market perception. There are so many Real Estate agents who are good at many things, but they are not excellent, or experts, at anything in particular. Multi-million dollar companies like Nike or McDonalds have logos and slogans, and they focus on being experts in their one target area. This has increased their value within their niche.

How many of us would like to be recognized as multi-billion dollar experts in our field? For you, **being an expert at a niche like condominiums or waterfront, or dealing with specific types of people like first-time buyers or seniors, could be a HUGE asset.** You should even consider certain neighborhoods or areas of your community, where you can try to become the resident expert. **Creating your own niche** will increase your perception levels in the market. It will help you stand out from your competition, by building your very own piece of the market.

Building your Niche

If you are proactive, you can build your own niche. You can pump up a certain area, call it an attractive name, and make people want to live there, because it is the new top neighborhood. There are countless ways to conquer a market niche, and the key to all of them is creativity. If you created the niche, who do you think people will come to when they decide they want to move there? You, of course!

People like to deal with experts in their field. Give that some thought and explore ways in which you can **become a brand within a certain niche** that suits you best. Learn to become recognizable at something and stand out from the crowd. You can never go wrong.

3

Open Houses

The open house that wasn't open

One day, I was showing property to a long-time client. We had finished up at the last house, and I suggested driving around the neighborhood to get a feel for it. The last house we had seen had an agent sign taped to the corner of the garage. After we were done, I was walking to my car, when a couple tentatively approached me. They said, "There is supposed to be an open house from 11 to 1pm here?" The man looked at me with hope in his eyes.

Since my clients were done, I picked up on their verbal and non-verbal clues and said, "If you want to see it, come on in!" I explained I was not the agent and told them what I knew, as I did have the MLS print-out. So, we proceeded back into the house. They wandered about, and I was not pushy; I believe in letting people work at their own pace. I had no more appointments that day, so I was free.

We talked for about 30 minutes, so, now it was close to 11:30. When they were done, they took my card and told me that, though they were looking for something, they were not ready to buy just yet. Then, they happily went on their way, after showing great appreciation for my having taken the time to talk to them. So, I proceeded to lock up, and the strangest thing was that the door kept opening when I tried to pull it shut. Exasperated, I finally just let it open... Lo and behold, another couple was there and, what did I hear again? You guessed right; they were also asking about the open house. This was a big house, and they had wandered in while I was with the other couple.

The couple chatted and chatted; they had no agent and were moving to the area. I gave them my last card. At that moment, to my utmost surprise, a third couple walked in, and the second couple chuckled and said, "You have to explain there really is NO open house." They had known all along that there really was no open house. All fired up and excited, I talked with this third couple about the market in general. They were investors, and we talked for some time. I ran out of cards, but the man wanted to make sure I had his email, name, and phone number. It was now close to 12:45. I was there almost the entire time for an Un-Open Open House.

But, what really happened after that? The investor saw a piece of property, liked it, and bought it with me. I continued to send information to the other two couples, and one of them bought property within 6 months of our meeting. Not bad for an Un-Open Open House Day!

Set your own rules

My own favorite method of prospecting is one which is completely underestimated and underutilized, namely, the Open House. I have wondered over the years who was it that set the rules that Open Houses had to be a minimum of two hours, or that they needed to be on afternoons or mornings, or only on certain days of the week.

Forget about closing times
One of the most powerful ideas I use in my own Open Houses is to only **advertise the houses as being open starting at a certain time**; for example "Open @ 1pm" or "Open From 1pm." **I would never advertise a fixed closing time.** If an Open House wasn't busy during

the first 45-60 minutes, it left me with the complete flexibility to shut down and move on to something else, and I could make more effective use of my time. I would encourage you to only advertise your Open Houses with a beginning time, as "open at" or "open from," and start with that strategy in place.

Show the neighbors first

Another great idea is to **have an open house for the neighbors**. One week prior to the Open House, you go around and invite the entire neighborhood to a **VIP neighborhood showing** of your listing. For one hour before your advertised open house, you can get all of the snoopy neighbors come through first, which allows you to focus on prospects during the actual Open House.

There are many benefits to this type of showing. You never know who might know somebody else who may want to buy in the area, and who is a better advocate of the area than the people who live there? The way to effectively do this is to knock on their doors and personally invite them to a one-hour neighborhood previewing, prior to your open house time. This is a good use of your time, as it may help you avoid wasting it on those nosy neighbors, when good prospects are coming through the Open House. I also find that **face to face time with neighbors is an excellent opportunity to add people to your sphere of influence.**

Control your open house

Another trick is to control the Open House. You can do this by placing a sign at the front door thanking people for their patience while you are showing the property. I control my environment and qualify my prospects by only allowing a few people through at a time. This way, I am able to look for one of the most important things that are often missed in an Open House: watching for buying signals; looking for the moments when somebody gasps or somebody starts imagining their furniture inside the house or gives that nudge to their spouse. These are all buying signals that you should be looking for during an Open House.

How easy is it to look for buying signals when you have ten people walking through a house all at one time? **Control your environment**, so you won't miss your sales and closing opportunities for that sit-down or a possible buyer/listing appointment. When you can focus on the clients you meet at the open house, you can build a rapport with them. This will be a lot more effective than having people running through the house, like a herd of cattle.

Create a buzz

The trick of controlling your environment has a double purpose. You are in the marketing business, **creating demand**, as there is a line-up forming at the front door. People have arrived early, because they don't know when you are closing the Open House, as you have not advertised a fixed time period. People are also waiting for you to show them the house one at a time, just like you experience at a busy new restaurant or a night club that just opened. You are creating a marketing buzz with all the people wanting to get in and see what all the interest is all about.

Now, you might think this is a bad idea, as some people might get impatient and just leave. I think the opposite is true; it is a great qualifying tool, because, if they are not serious about the house, they won't stick around. If they are dead serious about seeing what is inside the house, they will wait to get in, no matter what. Creating that sense of urgency and excitement is all part of your marketing strategy and what you are paid for by your sellers.

Keep your prospects guessing and keep them wanting to come through. My favorite situation is when somebody comes out of the house, as someone is going in, and someone else in the line says to his or her spouse, "those people look like they are really interested. If they buy this house before we go through, you are in trouble."

Sign the registry please!

In order to maximize the potentials of an Open House, you can **provide a guest registry**, where people who are viewing the house can leave their name and contact details. You can explain the reason for this to prospects, simply by saying that signing the book is a security feature, which has been requested by the home owner. At the very least, you will want names and either a contact phone number or an email address. You can also use this book as a qualifying tool, by refusing entry to anyone who is not prepared to sign the book. Just let the individuals know that the owner prefers not to have the house shown to people who refuse to give those basic details.

Protecting the Owners

Again, you might think this is a bad idea that could turn off potential buyers, but, from my own experience, I have had owners' belongings get damaged or go missing during an Open House. Not having a system in place to track the people who have come through the house leaves me completely helpless. It puts me in the position of not knowing who might be responsible for any loss or damage. On occasion, this has resulted in me having to compensate the homeowner for their loss; not a comfortable situation for anybody.

Presenting your message of benefits

What are agents saying at an Open House to encourage prospects to do business with them? Is it good enough to say you are a nice, hard-working agent who keeps in touch with clients? Do these words engage the client or set you apart from any other agent in the business?

You need to deliver a message of benefits. Prospects want to hear the answer to, "what's in it for me?" What are the benefits that prospects will get by doing business solely with you? Is it not good enough to be nice, work hard, or be honest? Come up with some benefits that will set you apart from your competitors and do answer the question of what's in it for prospective clients. For example, the benefit of having **confidentiality regarding their personal information:** Isn't there a benefit in sharing their personal information with only one agent? Wouldn't it make sense for them to only share their motivations and their personal/financial situation with one exclusive agent instead of sharing it with all kinds of agents?

What happens if your prospects share their personal information with multiple agents and then decide to go with one particular agent, putting in an offer through that agent? They will have lost most of their bargaining power, because the listing agent will also know all about their situation, as will any other agent who might be privy to the deal.

Here is a list of five benefits of doing business with one exclusive agent. I refer to this as my

Direct VIP Client Advantage

1. The Doctor/Patient Advantage
(Client Confidentiality)

Let's say you're going from house to house and agent to agent, sharing your personal and financial information with everyone. When you do put in an offer, how does it affect your bargaining power if the seller's agent already knows everything about you? It is critical that you share this information with only one agent, so that it won't work against you later. Your Buyer Agent is on your side, not the Seller's side.

2. The Instant Information Advantage
(No Communication Delays)

When you are relying on the internet, newspapers, or magazines as sources for house listings, their systems all have built-in delays, from a few days to a week, before the listing actually makes it to you. How many of the hottest deals or best buys make it that far before they are sold? Very few.

3. The Insider's Advantage
(Buyer, Meet Seller)

A great many hot pieces of property are sold exclusively by sleeve or pocket listings before they are even activated on MLS (Multiple Listing Service), well, before the public even knows about them. In these cases, the Sellers who wanted to sell and the Buyers who wanted to buy were introduced and made their transaction through the Direct Client program.

4. **The Inbox Advantage**
   (Convenient Email Updates)

As an agent, I have the technology to be notified of a new listing on the MLS system by the minute. I then quickly notify my Direct Clients. I can use my privileged access to this listing data to get you in to see your perfect home before most of the other potential Buyers even know about it.

5. **The Invisible Listing Advantage**
   (Find property that <u>isn't</u> for sale)

As part of a large sales force, I am constantly in contact with other agents. They may have Potential Sellers; home owners who would sell if they had a Buyer. We call this the water-cooler transaction. I mention I have someone looking for a special kind of property, and the other agent has a piece of property that fits like a glove, but isn't even on the market!

Staging

You may have already heard about staging. Staging means showing the home in such a way that the prospects go through an emotional experience, which encourages them to make a connection with the property.

People want the experience of buying something, not the experience of *being sold* something.

See the difference between the two? Why do they want to buy? Because buying anything makes us feel good. We love the thrill we get from buying. Who doesn't like to buy and spend money? It makes you feel good, and it can take away any negative feelings you might have had throughout the day.

The new Marketing IT

If you Googled "staging" five years ago, you would have found 300,000 results. Today, the search will yield over 2.75 million results. The fact is that, in the current market conditions, staging has become one of the fastest growing marketing tools in Real Estate. How many of you are incorporating staging into your presentations and marketing strategies? Ask yourselves: What do you like more; being sold something or being able to buy? What is it about buying that gets our mojo running? The central question here is; what triggers buying? The answer: EMOTIONS.

Triggering emotions

Staging is all about triggering EMOTIONS. Sellers are constantly asking, "What do I need to do to sell this house, other than giving it away by lowering my price?" **Start by providing your sellers with information on staging.** Stand out from your competition. Incorporate some expert knowledge of buyer behaviors and current market competition to develop a strategy to sell your clients` home by integrating pricing and staging.

Statistics show that buyers, when buying a home, make their decision based on the following characteristics:

Home Characteristics Influencing Buyer Choices

69%   **Location**

12%   **Curb Appeal**

10%   **Homey**

9%   **Size**

This means that 78% of the buyer's decision is already predetermined. You can't really do anything about location or size. We can only do something about Curb Appeal and Homey characteristics.

Regarding first impressions, statistics show that the most important things for prospective buyers are:

Aspects Influencing Buyers First Impressions	
Clean Clutter, Odor	35%
Décor	21%
Condition & Lighting	16%
Floor Plan	15%
Rooms	13%

This means that 72% of our buyer's first impressions can be controlled by the seller and the use of staging.

I once met a successful realtor who told me that she found that the most effective things to do in a home showing, besides cleanliness and décor, was having the smell of something baking in the oven or coffee. These are things that have a subconscious psychological effect on your buyers. You need to be aware of them and use them to your advantage.

Selling sellers on staging

Of course, staging will have a cost. It is unwise to tell your sellers that they will have to spend lots of time and money on staging. When you are facing this dilemma, I recommend using this dialog:

"Mr. and Mrs. Seller our goal is to have buyers feel the *spaciousness, well cared for, no work needed, perfect for their furnishings* emotions of *home sweet home.* Does this make sense?"

Now, since DE-CLUTTERING has such a huge impact, you need to focus on this in your staging. This can be a sensitive issue to address with home owners. I recommend using this dialog with them:

"De-cluttering your home is the key to the pricing process and triggering our buyers' emotions. To help with the process, I am providing you with complimentary boxes to get the process started. Buyers want to see the size of the rooms. They want to know that there is space for their things. I know there are valuable things for you in your house. Pack them up and keep them safe during the marketing process. You would hate to lose any of those precious memories or keepsakes."

Moving on to the next important factor affecting buyers' impressions, National Association of REALTORS® (NAR) reports that **67% of agent's don't feel comfortable talking about odor and cleanliness.** These may be sensitive points, but you need to find a diplomatic way of addressing them, as they are critical to pricing results.

I also advise **not having pets around** when showing a house. Again, to address this possibly sensitive issue, you could say something like, "moving and selling a home is stressful on a pet, just like it is on a child. How can we keep your pet safe and happy?"

Stylish & Neutral, that's the ticket

You need to make the house look as neutral as it possibly can. Light colors will help. Green, beige, and grey work very well. Allow the buyers to picture their furniture there. Give a spacey feeling. Cleaning, de-cluttering and stylish but neutral décor will do the trick. Bathrooms are very important. A clean odor, bright colors, fresh new towels, impeccable floor mats; you cannot underestimate the importance of these things.

In buyers' shoes

Ask yourself and your sellers these questions:

What does our audience care about?

What do they see?

What are they going to feel?

Become an expert on staging strategies in the eyes of your sellers to stand out from the competition. Provide valuable information on buyer behavior and the importance of integrating pricing and staging in today's challenging market. Dare to be different. Add to your value proposition and educate sellers on their responsibility for the final sale price too.

As you can see, it is crucial that you stage the house in such a way as to appeal to the buyers on an emotional level. If this is not something you are very good at, or if it is something you lack confidence in, you should get somebody else to do it. You want to create a special, evocative atmosphere in the house you are showing, which triggers positive feelings and emotions in your buyers, so that they will feel the urge to buy the property, without you having to *sell it* to them.

Handouts that won't end up in the trash

For example, quality handouts should be available for everyone that comes through the open house. Avoid the usual fact-sheet and business card handouts that are common in the industry. You need to stand out by creating great handouts that will engage people. They should include, for example; articles, market statistics, a list of the benefits of choosing a single agent, information on what is going on in the market and what is predicted for the future, and so forth. You may also include articles presenting valuable information about the return on investment of home renovations, and other similar topics, which may generate genuine interest in your prospective buyers.

Make An Impression!

This valuable information will engage your prospects, helping them remember their experience with you. Who are you most likely to remember? The agent who provides you with a fact sheet about the house and a business card or the one who has taken the time to put together some information like "the ten deadly mistakes a house buyer can make"? Think about what will make an impression on your prospects and be quick to provide it.

One house at a time

Here is another important tip; when you are conducting an open house, you **should only discuss the home that you are showing** at the moment. Remember that you will have an opportunity to close for a sit-down with your prospects, where you will have a chance to bring up other options and discuss their needs and expectations, at a later time.

I usually explain to my prospects that, out of fairness to the owners of my open house property, I concentrate on discussing the property being showcased, at that time. However, if prospects are not interested in the house you are showing, but they appear to be interested in buying or selling property, then you are creating a good impression, by offering to speak to them about their specific needs, on the occasion of a later appointment.

This provides you with the perfect excuse to **close for a later appointment** or sit-down with the prospects, and you are also creating a positive impression on them, because of the way you handled their request for information not related to the open house.

In order to keep building that crucial positive impression on potential customers, if I am asked a question that I don't know the answer to, I will tell them that I don't have the information they are looking for, but I will get it, if it is important to them. This technique will go a long way in building trust in the minds of your prospects. They will admire you for two things:

1. **You have the honesty to tell them the truth about not knowing the answers**

2. Your professional attitude in assuring them that you will make the effort to find out and provide the information they want

Asking the right questions

Exclusive Agent, anyone?

One question I often hear realtors asking is, "are you working with another agent?" I would recommend changing the wording of that question (which is, nonetheless, a crucial one) to something more like, "are you committed to another agent?" You will often get a question in return like, "what do you mean by committed?"

What you really need to know is whether your prospects are under contract with another agent, and this is a great way to engage in conversation with them about the benefits of an Exclusive Buyer Agent (EBA), what an Exclusive Buyer Agent Contract is all about, and how it can be beneficial to them.

Other power questions you can use can include these:

> ### *9 Simple Power Questions*
>
> **How long** have you been looking**?**
>
> **Have you seen** any homes you liked**?**
>
> **What has caught your eye** about this home?
>
> **How soon** do you want to move**?**
>
> **Where do you live** now**?**
>
> Do you **own or rent** property?
>
> **Is your home listed** or has it already been sold?
>
> Do you need to **sell before you buy?**
>
> Do you like this house **enough to buy it?**

Never forget to ask the prospect whether they actually want to buy the house they are looking at. If you don't ask them these questions, then you don't get the answers. Then, you might lose out on making business with the prospect, just by failing to ask the right questions.

Showing luxury homes

The last tip I would like to share with you in this section has to do with the high end luxury market. There is a fundamental difference between a regular open house and a high-end home showing: **you don't open house a high end product, you showcase it.**

This type of home will only invite an offer from equally high end individuals, and it might be a waste of time to do a regular open house. My solution is to do a special showcase in these cases.

The luxury home showcase

For example, you invite a jeweler, a clothier, a financial planner, a boat dealer, a luxury car dealer, and an RV dealer to bring all of the latest models of their products for a showcase at the high end house in question, for one evening. You ask them to contribute, explaining that their audience will be made up of an exclusive list of high net-worth people. You can ask them to contribute $500 for the privilege of showcasing their products in front of that very covetable potential audience.

Your Exclusive Guest List

Naturally, you assume that your sellers are high net-worth people themselves, who know and associate with other high net-worth individuals. Therefore, you can ask them for names and addresses that you can later use, to send out classy invitations to your showcase. The beauty of this system is that the showcase will be financed by the people you have invited, who have luxury products to offer this target market.

You provide cocktails, valet service, entertainment, catering, music, and high end luxury products on display. Over the course of the entire evening, your seller will be walking around endorsing you, introducing you to his high net-worth sphere of influence, actively promoting you in front of these people. This is an effective recipe for increasing your own sphere of influence, by spreading it towards the very market you wish to target.

4

Prospecting Methods

Farming

First of all, what is Farming? It is a method used to obtain prospects within a specific geographic area or product type like condominiums, or a specific type of prospects, such as first-time home buyers or senior citizens.

There are numerous available niches in farming, but the key is to know when it is advisable to farm a particular geographical area, product type or specific type of prospect. You need to find a niche which enjoys a considerable amount of business, a good turnover, and a large number of transactions.

Where to farm

For example, it would not be a good idea to be farming a product type that has no listings or sales or a type of prospect which does not participate in a significant number of Real Estate transactions. Take the time to **research which geographic areas are experiencing the most activity and sales** and go for them. Research the types of products that are generating the most transactions. Then, sit down and plan what type of farm area, product or person you are ready to focus on.

Once you have established a specific farming area or farming type, you need to understand the meaning of statistics. **It takes six separate contacts or touches, until a prospect or area perceives you as a dominant factor or expert in that specific area.** So, what are the things that you think you could possibly do, to create six separate touches or six separate contacts in a specific farming context?

A Farming Tale

A brand new agent and coaching client of mine moved from the big city to our smaller town to sell Real Estate. He was new to town and new to Real Estate. In fact, his background was in lottery outlet sales and he had no formal Real Estate experience whatsoever. He decided to take my advice and build a farming area.

We sat down and identified the area of town that had been experiencing the most listings and sales activity over the past year. We decided to farm that area of town. He sent out introduction letters to people living in the area, knocked on a bunch of doors each day and put a face to the name in his letter. He would send out area-market information, just listed, just sold notices; his activities would go on and on.

I remember a friend of mine who lived in the farm area mentioned to me that, at first he would get annoyed at seeing, reading, and hearing from my agent all the time, but after eight to ten months, he looked forward to what new information the agent would have about the market in the area. He actually said to me that, if he was going to do Real Estate business in the area, my agent would be at the top of his list. After consistently farming that area for a year, my agent was able to make a healthy six figure income, and he was recognized as the top expert in that particular niche. All from an agent who was new to both the area and the business! Such is the power of FARMING.

Know your village...

Of course, there is a way to make the farming process simpler than it was for my friend: **start in your own neighborhood.** This makes sense, because, who will know your neighborhood better than you do? You are comfortable in that area, and it is no problem for you to explain to people what you are doing and what your profession is.

I find that, time and again, most Real Estate agents don't get listings in their own neighborhood, because they tend to act a bit like secret agents. They have not taken the time to let people in their own home area know what their position is or what they might have to offer them. They would rather leave their neighborhood, allowing for someone else to come along and start trading in their own home area!

Meet the people

So, how do you get started? First, you **send out a letter of introduction**, explaining who you are and what the benefits of doing business with someone like you might be. You must focus on the value you can bring to people and the kind of information you can provide. Be sure to design this letter in such a way that it speaks directly to the prospects about their product, their neighborhood or about them on a personal level.

The next thing you need to do is **get face-to-face with them**. Put a face and name to that letter and establish a face-to-face rapport. Meet the people and introduce yourself to them. Ask them, "Do you have a trusted Real Estate professional that you would refer to friends or family? Do you have a relationship with them similar to the one you have with your family doctor, dentist or accountant? Do you have a Real Estate agent that you can trust for advice and information about your Real Estate needs?"

Pump up your benefits

If they answer in the negative, ask them whether that person can be you. Explain to them that, from time to time, you offer valuable information, and you are committed as their Real Estate information link. Tell them that you can provide valuable information on home renovations, buying and selling tips, improving credit score information, vacation ideas, and home maintenance ideas. If they are interested in this type of information, ask them where would be the best place to send it. On the other hand, if you had a hot Real Estate tip you would like to share with them, what would be the best number you could reach them at? Afterwards, spend the time to build that relationship and add the prospect to your database and sphere of influence.

Don't stop moving

Next, take the time to always **promote listings and sales statistics** in that specific area, or product type. Send out information to your prospects, so that they know you are keeping up-to-date with things that are happening in your specific niche area. This will allow you to establish your character and competency at the same time.

Sending out newsletters and using **phone follow-ups** (after you have got permission from the individuals, of course) are always powerful and efficient ways of building your niche. Let these newsletters and phone calls relate to statistics in that specific area and include other information relating to services, clubs, schools, as well as sporting and social events going on in the area.

Provide your farming area with a neighborhood or **product-specific website** that includes all sorts of information relevant to the people in your target niche. One example I saw recently was a website that focused entirely on military families and the information necessary for people in the military to buy and sell their homes.

Gifts that make a difference

Another great idea is to deliver small token gifts through celebrations and civic holidays; small pumpkins on Halloween, cinnamon hearts on Valentine's or chocolate Easter eggs during Easter. There are so many holidays throughout the year, which give you the opportunity to establish yourself in the neighborhood as someone who cares and knows what is going on there. This is how you can become the neighborhood expert.

You could also deliver useful promotional materials, such as business cards, pens, fridge magnets, mugs, and other similar items.

Based on statistics, the item that will elicit the most positive response from your customers is a fridge magnet. See that it contains useful emergency numbers, a calendar, an event-schedule, or something that will be of value to the prospects.

Keys to the kingdom

Once again, the key to the niche-kingdom is to create the perception that you are the go-to expert in that specific area or product type. You need to have multiple contacts, touches or connections with people before they will perceive you in this way. If you work diligently on your farming, you will find that you will have generated a lot of leads and listings over an 8 to 18 month period.

You will most likely come across many opportunities, in the course of your farming activities. You will realize that you have become that one person considered an authority on the listings or sales within your specific niche area.

Become a Farm Animal

Take the time to start building your farming activities today. Select your product type, area, or target market, starting by your own neighborhood. Get started on those activities that will, over the long term, build up your contact base and establish you as the "go-to-person" in your chosen area. The territory will provide a surge of business that, if nurtured, will never dry out.

5

Direct mail and Cold calling

Direct Mail

Over the years, I have seen many agents rely on direct mail as a prospecting method. Direct mail is an effective tool, but the question is, "are agents sending direct mail that will have value to the prospects, or are they sending direct mail that is of value to them?"

Standing out from the junk

At the end of the day, if direct mail is not answering the question, "what's in it for me?", then it holds no benefit to the prospects. Ask yourself this question; where do you normally find yourself opening your mail each day? The answer will probably be, "over the waste paper basket." Now, this is where most people open their mail. It is where they put mail they don't want. This is where most of your direct mail will go, unless people can see that it has a benefit or value to them.

Another important thing to remember about direct mail is that it is a complete waste, if it is not planned. Statistics show that **the percentage of effectiveness of direct mail is less than 1%.** It doesn't have any benefit to the receiver, as it is classed as junk mail.

In order to escape those grim statistics, you need to follow up your direct mail with either a personal appointment or a phone call.

Direct mail must have a form of value, so that it registers with the prospects and they consider it to be something worth reading and following up on.

Personal vs. Bulk

There are two different approaches to sending out direct mail. The first one is to send **personally addressed mail** to clients, contacts, and prospects. The second strategy is the bulk advertising approach, where you blitz out a lot of information to a specific area or group of people; this is known as the **shotgun method.**

An example of direct mail that is effective would be a "just listed" notice. While informing people that you have just listed a piece of property, you are also providing relevant information about the current prices of property on their own street, in their neighborhood, in their area of interest, or even in their own building. This is the kind of information that prospects will find interesting and valuable.

You can also use direct mail to **inform of your latest sales or to advertise upcoming open houses.** Another effective use of direct mail is when you **send specific information regarding a specific buyer that you are working with, and asking prospects in the area for their help.** You can describe your buyers and their demographics (i.e. where they work, if they have pets, children, etc.), explaining what they are looking for and asking for help in locating suitable property for them. Recipients tend to feel that they are getting more value from this type of direct mail, especially if they are in a position to help, through the contacts and people that they know.

The perfect newsletter

A monthly newsletter is another good piece of direct mail that may be perceived as valuable. It is also a **powerful client retention tool,** where you send out information and articles on Real Estate topics (home improvement, credit, identity theft protection, and things like that). You can include relevant statistics about Real Estate in your area and information pieces that will stimulate your prospects' interest and keep them reading the newsletter, month after month.

> ## What to include in a Newsletter
>
> **Pricing statistics**
>
> **Area sales statistics**
>
> **Home improvement tips**
>
> **Renovation ideas**
>
> **Credit & Mortgage info**
>
> **Just-listed / Just-sold notices**
>
> **Open House Announcements**

A newsletter does two things for you: it increases your competency in your business, showing prospects who you are as a professional, and it keeps you in contact with them. The newsletter serves as a prospecting tool, while it also reminds people that you exist. It keeps you at the top of their mind, at the times when you are not in direct contact with them.

Take out your quills!

Another powerful form of direct mail, which is underestimated and underutilized by most agents, is **the personal handwritten note**. A handwritten note, like a thank you note, is ALWAYS read. People always read them, because you have taken the time to write to them, and this has a very powerful effect. They make the recipient feel important, showing that you cared about them enough to write a personal note. **Never underestimate the simplicity and power of the personal note.**

Digital works too

Moving on from surface mail to the Internet, direct emails are also an effective method of contacting prospects. There is nothing wrong with using an electronic version of your newsletter or your "just listed" and "just sold" communications. Be sure to ask your prospects via which medium they prefer to receive your information. Some prospects will actually tell you, "both," depending on their lifestyle, but it is best to always ask your contacts what their preference is.

The Internet is in fact a great source of information for your Real Estate notes and newsletters. You can get input from magazine articles, blogs, press releases, social network pages, etc. As long as you give credit to the source of the information you are quoting from, you can use this information to add value to the direct mail you send out to your prospects.

Don't forget the **use of disclaimers.** Make sure you have a note somewhere on your direct mail that says that you are not soliciting anything and that you are not representing yourself as an authority in law or accounting (for example). Make sure that each piece of direct mail also gives prospects instructions on how to discontinue your information services.

The good old detachable form

I have also found that direct mail gives you a great opportunity to include something extremely useful, namely, a detachable form to be filled out by prospects and returned to you. Encourage people to do this, in exchange for a free subscription to your newsletter or a free appraisal; whatever you come up with that can be of value to them. Having a section of your direct mail that prospects can fill out with their details and send back to you increases the "stick-ability" of your direct mail, because it boosts interaction.

It's not about you, it's about them

Direct mail is invaluable, but it should not be about you. People don't care whether you are number one or if you have done this or that. What they want are pieces of information that can be of value and interest to them, on a personal level. I cannot stress enough how important it is for any piece of direct mail to **include something of value for the prospect.** Once, I sent out direct mail using the shotgun approach, mailing more than 10,000 people. Strangely, I did not receive a single listing, nor any calls from buyers, or anything at all. It was because the direct mail was about me and what I could do for them, not about what benefits prospects would get from doing business with me. That may appear to be a subtle difference, but it is a crucial one.

"Cold" Calling

The days of cold calling are over. Thanks to the current legislation, you can't just go phoning people whenever you want, especially if you do not know them prior to making the call. The numbers for most people are available from many sources, for example, reverse listing directories. However, just because the information is available, it does not mean that you can use it in any way you want. Even if you could make cold phone calls to people you don't know, your lead capture rate is only going to be between 1 and 10%. That is not a good return for your time investment. If you want to do any type of cold calling, I recommend you do it face-to-face.

"Warm" Calling

When you make the calls to people you actually know, there are some basic steps you need to follow. Give a brief introduction first, and then provide valuable information for the client, so that they see some value in your call. It does not necessarily have to be directly about Real Estate, but it has to deal with a related topic. Please make sure that the information you are giving is as relevant as it can possibly be for the person you have called; a listing or sales price in their area for example. Something like that will get you a better response than just calling to tell them about your business.

Asking prospects for help

One of the most effective "warm" calls you can make is when you are trying to source a property for a buyer. If you call people you don't know, but who are in the area that the buyer is interested in, you will be amazed at the number of people who really respond to being asked for their assistance. They will probably give you the life story of virtually everybody on their street, in an effort to find you the type of property you are looking for.

Going Face to Face

You can do something similar with door-to-door campaigns. Make sure that the information you have is specific and relevant to the area you are canvassing. Alternatively, you can ask people whether they are aware of any property that might be suitable for your buyer's specific needs. You can also use the door-to-door approach to invite neighbors to preview your open houses.

Body language control

The key to being successful at door-to-door and face-to-face prospecting is to always be enthusiastic and passionate about your topic, and to wear a smile on your face. Don't forget that your body language and use of eye contact are really important. Have a planned dialog that you are comfortable with, which sounds natural and seems to flow, so that people quickly become engaged in what you are saying.

When somebody answers the door, always step back a few steps, so that you are not making them uncomfortable, by invading their space. Turn slightly away from them, so you are projecting a more open approach. After they open the door, compliment them on their driveway, their garden, house color, or whatever else you can say and still appear genuine about it.

Dale Carnegie (the master of writing to improve your self-confidence) was famous for saying that…

**THE MOST EFFECTIVE WAY TO WIN PEOPLE OVER
IS TO ALWAYS GREET THEM WITH A SMILE
AND A COMPLIMENT**

Sound simple? Then, just go ahead and do it!

Personal Security

You do have to consider your own personal security, if you decide to go door-knocking. Watch out for dogs, especially. Carry a whistle with you, or a cell phone to have some safety mechanism on you. Make sure that somebody always knows where you are and what time you are expecting to leave a specific area. You should make arrangements to phone in and touch base with somebody by a specific time, so that, if something does happen to you, there will be somebody who can raise the alarm on your behalf. Another alternative is to work in pairs; with each one of you doing one side of the street. It is a sad but true fact that times have changed, and you cannot take your own personal security for granted anymore, so make sure you are keeping yourself as safe as you possibly can.

More Names, No Push

If you are door-knocking, do not forget to take the opportunity to capture contact details for your database. Remember the key questions outlined earlier: "do you have a Real Estate person that you use and recommend to others, much like you would a doctor, accountant or lawyer?" If the answer is "no", then ask them if you can be that person. If somebody asks you why you want their contact details, or why you think they need a Real Estate professional, you can let them know that you do send valuable information out to your contacts.

Don't forget to get a phone number from them, so that you can contact them if you have hot property deals coming up in the near future or some relevant time-sensitive piece of information, which would be best conveyed over the phone. This is what is known as a "soft sell" approach, and it is a great way for you to get new contacts for your database, without using any pushy sales techniques.

6

Opportunities

Expired Listings

Let's consider expired listings. Expired listings are a key area of opportunity in both the balanced and struggling markets. In the current market, if 32% of listings are selling, 68% of all listings are going off the market as unsold. What an incredible opportunity to gain from! Statistics say that 85% of these items will be listed again with another Real Estate company.

> **LISTING STATS**
>
> Listings that **Sell**   32%
>
> Listings going off **Unsold**   68%
>
> Unsold Listings that will be **Active again 85%**

Why are expired listings a tremendous opportunity offered to you on a platter: because the owners of the property already want to sell. They are already prepared to pay real estate commission fees, and

85% of these prospects are looking to list again with another Real Estate professional. Can you see the **powerful opportunity** that comes from expired listings now?

However, there are a few considerations to take into account. First and foremost, make sure that the property listing has been checked as being off the market and that it has contractually expired. You do not want to cut into somebody else's active listings, because that would be a breach of business ethics.

Breaking the realtor-phobia

Here is a big concept you need to understand. You have to remember that **the last person a dejected home seller wants to see at their doorstep is a Real Estate agent,** because they think that their agent let them down and didn't sell their house the first time around.

So, you have to be an **empathetic, sympathetic listener** to these folks. I use the analogy that the expired listings are like a giant red helium balloon, which is about to pop. How do you make a giant red helium balloon more manageable? You let out a little air to deflate it. So, in order to get these owners to put their guard down, you should ask them questions that let them get their hot air out.

The question is **how do you begin to get these owners to vent and deflate?** Talk about the competition without even knocking them. What do I mean by that? That means you need to ask them questions about their last Real Estate experience and about their last agent. For example, the line I like to use is, "We have just been notified that your property is now off the market. I was looking at the statistics and information and I cannot believe that this property did not sell." Obviously they are going to feel the same way, so this is a good time to ask them, "Why do you think it did not sell?"

Your job is to listen

Get prepared, with pen and paper, and write down their responses. Listen to what they are saying; ask them about their communication experiences with their last agent. Ask about their marketing campaign; what kind of online marketing campaign was used and what kind of showing and feedback system did they have in place.

If you listen to their answers, trying to capture what the last agent didn't do, you are going to let the steam out of the red helium balloon to soften your prospects up. Once they have vented, review quickly what their last agent did or did not do and confirm that this is the right information. Then, find a way to let them know that you are an expert at selling hard-to-sell property. Later, you can ask them, "well, if I can ensure that the same mistakes are not repeated and I offer you my platinum marketing proposal to list your house and get it sold this time, would you be interested?"

That is the closing question. That is how you establish the engagement. Why not go after someone who wants to relist; someone who already wants to pay commission and is ready to sell? There is a tremendous opportunity with the 68% of unsold listings, why not go after those opportunities?

I find that many Real Estate agents assume that other realtors are going after these expired listings, but I am here to tell you that less than 10% of agents in most areas will go after expired listings at the outset. Even then, none of them will last longer than the second or third week of follow up.

It is all about the initial contact, following up, engaging the dejected sellers, and showing them that you are someone who cares. You have to be empathetic and let them know that you specialize in property that is hard to sell. **Show them that you won't have their previous realtor's shortcomings and that you are the person who can get their property sold this time.**

For Sale by Owner

The next opportunity is the "For Sale by Owner" category, which can be a hugely attractive sector. Again, 80-90% of them will list with an agent, if they are unsuccessful in selling their property themselves.

I love the psychological approach of understanding that you are going to help for-sale-by-owner prospects sell their house themselves. You are probably thinking to yourself right now, "what? Is he crazy? You are going to help these people sell their own property themselves?" The answer is yes.

Helping owners with direct sales

Let's face it, who wouldn't want to save thousands of dollars in agent's commissions, by selling themselves? Don't say you wouldn't. They are all going to try it, at the outset.

Understand that you are in the business to help people buy and sell Real Estate. You are going to help these people. Initially, **you are going to give them information that will help them sell their houses themselves.** You will get out of the office and drive around and go face-to-face with these people and give them a **complimentary information package.**

EXPIRED LISTING FACTS

80-90% will list with an Agent

Average time before they list: **10 weeks**

Statistics say that it takes an average of 10 weeks for an owner to give up trying to sell themselves and consider listing the property. So, for one day a week, over the course of 10 weeks, you will call in at their house, bringing them useful tools, to help them sell their house.

Draft up mock advertising and marketing campaigns to show them one week. Give them a market evaluation another week. Give them a showing feedback guest registry book or tips on staging the home for selling the next week.

Each week, you are dropping off an item that will help them sell their house themselves. Understand that the owner will ask you,

"Why are you doing all these things for me?" The answer is "I am in the business of helping people buy and sell Real Estate and I can see that you are in the market to sell your property." Don't tell them they are going to die, that they can't, that they are crazy or that they won't sell it themselves. Why use fear tactics? Why not help them do it and see what you can end up doing?

TOOLS TO HELP WITH "FOR SALE BY OWNER"

"For Sale by Owner" Sign
(With Your Name and Logo on the Bottom)

Complimentary Contracts

Generic Feature Sheets

Photos of the Property (Taken With Their Permission)

Mock up Marketing Campaigns

Market Evaluation

What you will find is that after a number of weeks, if they are not successful in selling their property, they are certainly going to be ready to list with an agent. And, when they are ready to do that, what are the chances of them listing with you after all that you have done for them? There is probably a 90-100% chance.

If they successfully sell the house themselves, in a lot of cases, they will be in the market to buy. Chances are that 80-90% of the time they will use you to buy, because they feel that you have given them something with no expectation of a return. They will feel as though they are indebted to you and will therefore want to return the favor.

Along my career, I have found that, if somebody sells their property themselves with my help, they will later buy another piece of property with me. Not only will they buy with me, but they will send

5 or 6 buyers or sellers over to me, over the course of the following twelve months.

That is how powerful this system is. So, keep records, keep notes, follow up, go back each week, and give them another item of value. Understand that this is another tremendous opportunity for you, which very few other agents will actually take advantage of. Agents will send out direct mail, but why not go to the owners face-to-face and give them something of value to help them sell, and then work with them?

I hope that you can now comprehend the power of working with For-Sale-by-Owner and Expired listings property. The opportunities are tremendous.

7

Managing your time

Filling the Jar

One day, a time management expert was speaking to a group of students. To drive home a point, he used an illustration the students would never forget. As he stood in front of them, he said, "Okay, time for a quiz." He then pulled out a one-gallon, wide-mouthed masonry jar and set it down on the table in front of them. Then he produced about a dozen fist-sized rocks and carefully placed them, one by one, inside the jar. When the jar was filled to the top and no more rocks could fit inside, he asked, "Is the jar full?" Everyone in the class said "Yes."

After that, he said "Really?" He then reached under the table and pulled out a bucket of gravel. He dumped some gravel in and shook the jar, causing pieces of gravel to work themselves down into the space between the big rocks. Then he asked the group once more. "Is the jar full?" By this time the class was on to him. "Probably not," one of them answered. "Good!" he replied. He reached under the table and brought out a bucket of sand. He started dumping the sand into the jar and it went into all the spaces left between the rocks and the gravel. Once more he asked the question. "Is the jar full?"

"No." the class shouted. Once again, he said, "Good!" then he grabbed a pitcher of water and began to pour it in until the jar was filled to the brim.

Then, the time management expert looked at the class and asked, "What is the point of this illustration?" One student raised his hand and said, "The point is that, no matter how full your schedule is, if you try really hard, you can always fit some more things into it." "No," the speaker replied, "that's not the point."

"The point is," he continued, "that if you don't put the big rocks in first, you will never get them in at all. What are the big rocks in your life? (Your children, your spouse, your loved ones, your friends, your education, your dreams, a worthy cause, teaching or mentoring others, doing things that you love, time for yourself, your health etc.) Remember to put these Big Rocks in first, or you will never get them in at all."

The lesson is that, if you sweat the little stuff (i.e. gravel, the sand), then you will fill your life with little things. You will never have the real quality time you need to spend on the big, important stuff; the big rocks.

Finding Your Big Rocks

So, tonight or in the morning, when you are reflecting on this short story, ask yourself this question: What are the big rocks in my life? Then put those in your jar first. Remember: it is you who decides what the BIG ROCKS are, not someone else.

Top agents are constantly focusing their time on high-dollar activities. They are asking themselves "is what I am doing right now going to make me a listing, a sale or a high return on my time investment?" Some of the things that they do are practicing their dialogs daily, role playing, and listening to other top people in the business. If you want your business to grow, then you have to grow your skills. If you do not, then you are dying in this business.

What gets you going

If you have no plan, direction, or purpose, then you do not know what you are growing towards. One of the most important skills I have developed is having goals or a vision board. The vision board is a powerful technique, where you put a bulletin board together (or a screensaver or something that you will see every day) that has visuals and photos of things that really get you excited; things you are passionate about. They have to be things that remind you of why you work so hard and why you do what you do. This will motivate you and give you energy. Have that vision board handy and focus on the reasons why you do what you do every day.

Invest money on keeping your clients, building the relational side of things, and carrying out those relational activities. Having client appreciation events, having different opportunities where you pop in and visit people and give them items of value; these are important things you need to focus on. Don't be afraid to give people little tokens of your appreciation and let them know that they are important to you. You want to be in front of these people and let them know that you care.

Time blocking

The single most powerful activity that I attribute my success in time management to is "time blocking". Jim Rohn said, "You need to finish your week before it begins." What he means by that is that, unless you take control of your week before it begins, then something else or someone else will. Before your week starts, maybe on Sunday evenings, take your day planner and slot in your two or three hours of prospecting time each day.

You can also slot in your caravan[8] and your tour days. Block out your appointments with family, friends and spouses. Block out time for yourself. This leaves pockets of time open that you can allocate to unscheduled appointments for listings or sales. You can offer

---

[8]   This is where a group of different agents visit several listings in a particular area. Their input and different perspectives can give you a fresh approach on selling a home.

people options of times that suit them, based on the pockets of time you have open throughout the week.

Don't worry that people are going to be put off by you being successful and having much of your time already allocated. They will be glad when they can meet with you. Time blocking is a powerful way of showing people that you are successful and in demand.

The cell phone dilemma

Think about this, can you reach your successful doctors, lawyers or accountants on their cell phone? Why should you always be available to answer your cell phone? When you are constantly answering your cell phone, you are sending a message to people that you may not be successful, because you always answer your phone. Here is an alternative method. It is called **real-time voice messaging**. Create a voice message asking people to leave their messages when they call you. Let them know on your message what times you are available to return their calls. You have to protect you integrity and build trust with these people by phoning them back, whenever you said that you would.

I find that, when realtors are working with buyers and answering their phone, they are not only sending a message to the caller that they are not busy, but, more importantly, they are sending a message to the buyer that they are not really that important. With these actions, we sabotage ourselves in Real Estate. You send a message to people that you really don't care about them, only about yourself or the person on the other end of the line.

So, how are you doing?

One of the last things you need to figure out is how you should respond, when people are asking you how things are. Saying things like, "oh, I am busy," "crazy busy," or "can't even keep up," may have a negative impact on your business. If somebody cares about your well-being and all they hear is how busy you are and how overwhelmed you are with work, do you think they will be giving you another piece of business, or another referral? No way.

If you present yourself this way, the last thing they will want to do is send you another piece of business and end up causing you a nervous breakdown, or causing your marriage to fall apart. Be more careful and aware when you are answering questions like this, because you might underestimate the negative effects this type of communication could have on your business. It is a self-sabotaging activity; pure and simple.

In a nutshell, use time blocking to ensure that you use your time efficiently and you know what you spend your time doing. Have control over your time, rather than relinquishing it to somebody else. Take control of your phone and cell phone time, scheduling it like everything else, and you will be less likely to sabotage your own business.

Goal setting

A young man asked Socrates the secret to success. Socrates told the young man to meet him near the river the next morning. When they met, Socrates asked the young man to walk with him toward the river. When the water got up to their neck, Socrates took the young man by surprise and ducked him into the water. The boy struggled to get out, but Socrates was strong and kept him there until the boy started turning blue.

Socrates pulled his head out of the water and the first thing the young man did was to gasp and take a deep breath of air. Socrates asked, "What did you want the most when you were there?" The boy replied: "Air." Socrates said: "That is the secret to success. When you want success as badly as you wanted the air, then you will get it. There is no other secret."

The motivation to succeed comes from the burning desire to achieve a purpose. Napoleon Hill wrote:

> "Whenever the mind of man can conceive and believe, the mind can achieve."

I believe in a 90 day goal plan. Focus on these five different areas of life over 90 day time periods:

GOALS OF THE 90-DAY PLAN

- **You**: Focus on activities that help you improve and develop yourself, such as reading, quiet time, alone time or prayer.

- **Relationships**: What do you want regarding your family and friends? Block times and dates when you want to focus on these relationships and plan specific activities for them.

- **Business**: How are you going to manage your business activities? What do you want to achieve and where do you want your business to be?

- **Finances**: What do you want to accomplish financially? What are your financial goals?

- **Spiritual**: How do you want to keep yourself in a positive state of mind and spirit?

These are important things that you need to set goals for and focus on for each 90 day period, reviewing them every 45 days. If you accomplish some or all of them within those 45 days, you reset the goals for a further 90 day period.

Ensure that you have a business plan, that you set goals, and that your vision board is in place. Complete your time blocking and make sure you take time off, by writing these things down in your day planner or your electronic PDA.

People can sense it when you need some time off or when you are desperate to make a sale. People can also sense it when you are enjoying what you are doing. So, have passion, have fun, and love what you do. Remind yourself that Real Estate is the world's greatest business, because there is no ceiling to your income potential, you have unlimited freedom with your time, and you get more back out of Real Estate than what you put in. There is no other business that has these same opportunities.

Keeping control

However, many people are not wise with the responsibility that comes with **freedom of time and self-accountability.** They are sometimes not wise with their income and they lose control of it, spending more than they make. They don't understand that income must exceed outgoing funds. These are common areas, where people in Real Estate fail on a regular basis. So, don't plan to fail, but have a plan and focus on it.

A personal friend of mine shared a story with me about having lunch with a top producer in Real Estate. My friend asked the top producer "how are you doing?" The top producer nodded and smiled while eating his lunch and said "business is fantastic, the market is strong, things couldn't be better."

My friend sat there for a minute and asked the top producer again, "how are you really doing?" The top producer stopped for a second, looked at my friend and said, "you really want to know how I'm doing?" My friend said "yes, how are you really doing?" The top producer replied "it is crazy to think that in a few hours I am about to get on stage and share my success with hundreds of other agents and tell them how to be just like me. The truth is that I am about to file for personal bankruptcy, my wife has left me, and she has taken my 2 children with her. My life is a complete mess." My friend sat with the top producer and told him that he had heard the same story from many top producers in the business,

This is why I cannot stress enough, how important **managing your goals** can be for your business, for your family, and for every aspect of your personal life that you care about. No plan, no gain. If you don't plan ahead, things will just fall on your head, and it will be too late. Use the 90-day planning slots, or any other timeframe that works for you. Keeping track of your use of time and your goals is the only way to stay ahead in every aspect of your life, be it spiritual, romantic, social, or financial.

8

Going from Good to Great

High on a hilltop overlooking the beautiful city of Venice, Italy, there lived an old man who was a genius. Legend had it that he could answer any question anyone might ask of him. Two of the local boys figured they could fool the old man, so they caught a small bird and headed for his residence.

One of the boys held the little bird in his hands and asked the old man if the bird was dead or alive. Without hesitation the old man said, "Son, if I say to you that the bird is alive, you will close your hands and crush him to death. If I say the bird is dead, you will open your hands and he will fly away. You see, son, in your hands you hold the power of life and death."

In *your* hands, you hold the seeds of failure or the potential for greatness. Your hands are capable, but they must be used for the right things, to reap the rewards you are capable of attaining. What are the two most important words in sales? The first important word in sales is the word "you." Many salespeople believe that customers buy their products first, but the reality is that the first sale is "you."

Selling yourself

You sell yourself. A client must believe in you and like you and your message. Have you ever walked out on a pushy sales person and come back later to buy the same product from someone that you liked? You also bought the salesperson.

How is your personal product? How is your "you"? Is it salable or does it need work? Being the best that you can be and believing it is vital to sales and sales success.

The second important word in sales is the word "why." It is important, because it leads to one thing: answers. You can't make sales without answers. You need answers to "why you," "why them," and "why ask."

Let's examine each one of these questions in depth:

Why you?

Why are you in sales? Not just to make money. It is for the things that you will do with that money, what that money will buy you and how it will help you. I challenge you to find the reason "why" you are in sales. Remember on a daily basis what your why is. As the old proverb says, "with a big enough <u>why</u>, the <u>how</u> takes care of itself."

Why them?

The biggest mistake salespeople make is to sell for their own motives. You need to sell for the customers' "why" first. Once you find out what their "why" is, you can sell them on it.

Why ask?

Questions are the hardest skill to perform in sales. To get the right answers, you have to ask the right questions. Have pre-planned powerful questions, test them for reaction, and test them for responses.

In Real Estate sales, it is important that you remind yourself daily that it is not you that people are rejecting but your service and that your service might not be something that they need at this time. That does not mean they won't require it another time.

Be aware of your struggles, your disappointments and when you are starting to burn out. Remind yourself daily that if anyone can, you can. I have learned over the years that there is nothing special about successful people. Successful people deal with the same things that you do, 24/7. You need to believe in yourself. The thing you need to focus on the most is that, no matter how hard things may get, you need to persevere.

The learning curve

"From birth, up until the time we are about eighteen, our learning curve is dramatic, and our capacity to learn during this period is just staggering. We learn a tremendous amount very fast. We learn language, culture, history, science, mathematics...everything! For some people, the accelerated learning process will continue on. But for most, it levels off when they get their first job."

Jim Rohn

A requirement for success is education. I mean the practical education you get by application. Education without application is completely worthless. Apply what you learn on a daily basis, in sales and in life. We are not successful by just attending a 2-hour seminar; we must apply what we have learned from that seminar, in order to change our life.

Like Jim Rohn said, it almost looks as though adults stop learning after they are 18, or they guess that they have arrived and don't need to do it anymore. This is a very interesting state of things, for a number of reasons.

Why do we stop being students and why don't we continue learning? There is a Buddhist proverb that says, "When the student is ready, the master will appear." You need to understand that your education is internalized; more importantly, it is applied. It is the combination of education and application that you can expect to get results from.

LEARNING FACTS

Real Estate agents earning $250,000+ gross income each year **invest an average 10% on education and training.**

Agents earning less than $150,000 gross income per year **invest an average of 1%** or less on education and training.

DREAMS

Over the last 100 years, in Real Estate, everyone has had high expectations. People believe that they are going to get their license, a new car, a cell phone, and make lots of money; happy ending.

REALITY

Only 50% of those who buy the Real Estate course actually finish it.

Only 50% of those who finish actually pass the exam.

Only 50% of those who pass are still in the business after their first year.

The reality is that, **once you buy the Real Estate course you have about a 33% chance of remaining in the business after the first year.** That means that only one out of four people are surviving in this business. If this business is so easy, as most people believe, then why are the success statistics so low?

Be aware that the market will go up and the market will come down. It always has and it always will. But, in every market, there is an opportunity. You have to be aware of those times when high interest rates come into play, as supply will exceed demand and homes will be worth less than what was paid for them. There have always been correctional times during the cycles in the past years. It will go up and down, you just need to be aware of current trends and prepare for them.

Statistics say that **1 out of 10 agents in this business do great.** They do better and better every year, no matter what the market conditions are. **2 out of 10 agents get to good, but they don't ever go from good to great.** They put in the time, but they never really understand what it takes or how to get to that next level. Lastly, 7 out of 10 agents stay static. They don't know how to handle the ups and downs and the constant mood swings of the business and they end up quitting. They just choose to get out of the business. In which category do you want to be?

Winners never quit, quitters never win

"Everyone would like to be the best, but most organizations lack the discipline to figure out with egoless clarity what they can be the best at and the will to do whatever it takes to turn that potential into reality. They lack the character and the discipline to rinse their cottage cheese."

"Good to great"

Jim Collins

I see so many agents in their second, third or fourth year tripping into the office once in a while, listing a few items at random prices, and working with lookers or buyers. They may still be making some money, but, for some reason, they have stopped doing those activities that grew their business. Why are we such creatures of habit that we stop thinking that we have to do the basic activities or work hard at this business?

Why do agents stop doing those activities that make them money? I see many agents that are stuck in a rut. When I was in their shoes, whenever I found myself staring at a rut, I would remind myself to get back to the fundamentals and get back to basics. I would just get out and see the people. In Real Estate, we are in the relationships business and we need to get in front of people who need our help.

Discipline can go a long way

Some people just become apathetic and complacent, not wanting to do those things known as work, W O R K, the things that take time and effort. As Jim Collins put it, the main things they lack are discipline, discipline, and discipline.

Someone who is outstanding in Real Estate is someone who is focused, disciplined, and constantly improving. These are individuals who have people, systems or mechanisms in place, to hold themselves accountable in the business.

Escaping the Vortex

Beware of the one deal vortex, where you are spending all of your time and effort on just one big deal. Meanwhile, time is passing and your money is running out. A closing in Real Estate is not what time the office door is locked. Closings are sales and transactions. They are signatures on listings and sales documents; the key indicators of our success.

Don't put in twelve-hour days seven days a week and earn a poverty income. Don't become the undertaker in Real Estate, where you drive people around in your car until they sign or die. Ask yourself, **"Is what I am doing right now going to make me money?"**

Who is responsible for people failing in Real Estate? This may be a strange question to answer, coming from a Real Estate broker, but I believe that agents, Real Estate managers, and their brokers are responsible. Find someone who will not allow you to have the option to fail. Statistics say that if we give someone the option to fail, 70% of agents will take that option and bow out, instead of pressing on.

This is a business that is easy to get into. It is also easy to get out of. **If agents are given the option to get busy or get out, 70% will get out, because they don't believe in themselves and feel that no one else believes in them.** Self-esteem is the number one killer for agents getting out of the business, because if you don't buy yourself, then nobody else will buy you.

Taking control

Why do so many agents never get to great? The number one reason is that **they are not taking control of buyers or sellers,** by focusing on learning how to qualify them quickly, by building a rapport with them, establishing a timeline, and identifying their motivation levels.

Another reason most agents remain on a mediocre level is that they fail to surround themselves with positive people in business, positive people in their organization, and positive people in their daily lives. On the other hand, they don't realize that they need to focus their efforts on high dollar, high priority activities, so they won't end up burned out and in financial trouble.

Great agents take control and focus on high dollar activities. We all have the same 24 hours and the same 7 days in a week. It is what **we are doing with our time that makes all the difference.** In Real Estate there are certain areas that we need to consider, if we want to be good and then great. What does it take to go out and get a listing on any given day? It takes skills. Contacting your close friends or family to list their house doesn't take skills.

It takes skill to obtain a listing from a for-sale-by-owner or an expired listing prospect. How do you get skills in Real Estate? By learning the skills first and then applying them. You get better and better each and every time. **Celebrate your successes and learn from your failures,** as they will help you refine your skills and lead you to greater success.

Good News, The Wheel has been invented.

Move on!

The next area to consider is technique. Why is it that 80% of agents shy away from technique, dialogs, and scripts? Some agents' say that they don't need to work on these areas, because they don't want to sound canned. I say, don't sound canned, but, in sales, you have to sound planned. Over the last 100 years, the best people in this business have already said it all.

So, why not learn from what they have said? Why not internalize scripts and dialogs and make them sound like your own? Why try to re-invent the wheel? Some of us rely on our exterior appearance and personality, but we don't work enough on skills, techniques, and dialogs. How far do you think that will take you?

Let's consider our attitudes. Your attitude needs to include thoughts like, **"if anyone can, I can" and "someone is listing with me today, because they need me and they will be glad they did," or "someone is going to buy today, they just don't know it yet."** Attitude is the key, but it is not the only key. If I had an agent who was an idiot, for example, and I motivated him, then what would I have? I'd have a motivated idiot. So, you can see that attitude cannot compensate for certain kinds of shortcomings, but it is still essential.

All about Ink on Paper

How do we measure our success in Real Estate? You know you are getting results in this business when you are getting signatures. Measure your success by the number of signatures you are getting on listing contracts, sales contracts, exclusive buyers` agency contracts, and fee agreement contracts. These signed documents determine your production results in Real Estate.

Inventory Rules

Going from good to great also involves always controlling your listing inventory, as getting listings will give you lasting power.

Control your sales inventory, since you need to be ahead of the sales curve for the future. Don't play catch up. Instead, plan your sales one month, two months, and three months ahead. This way, you don't have to worry about when your dollar is coming, finding yourself under pressure and having to force a sale. Keep track of your attitude, making sure and reminding yourself that: "if anyone can, I can," and "there is nothing special about special people; the difference is only what they do."

The 3-Part Formula for Success

1. Get a salable listing

There is a three part formula for success in Real Estate. The first part of the formula is about obtaining a salable listing every week. I don't mean just any listing, but a listing that will sell. Listings are the name of the game, because if you don't list, you don't last. All top producers have one thing in common: a large well-priced listing inventory.

2. Qualify Buyers & Sellers

Part two is learning how to qualify buyers and sellers. Learn how to separate lookers from buyers and sellers from dreamers. The number one time waster in the Real Estate business is focusing on people who are not motivated or not qualified. A buyer needs two things when they get into your vehicle: a check book and a measuring tape. The check book is for them to put a deposit on a house they are purchasing today and the measuring tape is to see if their furniture is going to fit.

3. Find Motivated Sellers

Part three addresses the seller and their motivation. What is their motivation? What is their reason for selling? Ask them, "what will you do, if you do not sell," and then listen to their answer. If they don't have a response for that, you don't need to go any further with them for now, because they don't need to sell. Walk away from the listing. Find the sellers that want to be **in the market** and not **on the market**. There is a big difference.

9

Pricing Strategies

"If you're not worried that you're pricing it too cheap, you're not pricing it cheap enough."

Roy H. Williams

Though the above statement by Williams may seem extreme, the mistake of pricing too high tends to happen more often than that of pricing too low, hence the need to be vigilant. When it comes to pricing Real Estate, connecting is the key. You must connect with your sellers early in the pricing process. You need to try to understand what their challenges and emotions are.

Connecting with your sellers

The first thing you need to ask them is, "what kind of challenges do Mr. and Mrs. Seller foresee in marketing your property?" Their expected challenges could be waiting, high expectations, they paid too much for their home, they need/want too much, or the fact that there is too much inventory and competition.

After you have established where they stand in this respect, ask them what kind of emotions they think they will be encountering, throughout the selling process. For example, anger, frustration, guilt, or resentment. Going through the connection process with the seller is incredibly important to pricing.

When you start to establish price with sellers, **never use the word price.** Why? Psychologically, price refers to worth or value. Therefore, the word price gives the seller false expectations. **The only time price is really established and identified is at closing time**, when they receive their money. **Switch your wording from "pricing" to "positioning."**

> **Lead generation is like a Ferris wheel; you bring people on as you move people off**

Positioning Homes

We have to find a position for homes, in comparison to other ones that are in the market. By using the word "position" instead of "price," you avoid building those false expectations. You must visually identify the seller's home in terms of the competition and what its position is in the market.

At this stage, realtors usually make a competitive marketing analysis (CMA). You should switch your wording to a **"qualified home assessment"** or a **"market positioning for homes."** Using these phrases instead of CMA is more attractive to your sellers, and it shows them that you are someone who might be doing things differently. Remember: successful people are no different, but they do things differently.

Sellers are only interested in people who are qualified buyers. So, think about this: buyers only look for qualified homes. The sellers` home must qualify in order to be shown and sold. The question is where will the home qualify (in terms of price) for a loan? Would this be a good starting point?

The only way a seller can truly establish value for their home is by keeping it. Do you think that is a fair comment? As agents, we set them up with false expectations. So, change the wording from price to positioning. Create a home property assessment or a property positioning and change the way we are talking about pricing in Real Estate.

There are really only two things we can do for sellers; we can predict buyers` responses and advise them on how to deal with them. By doing this, you can create excitement and urgency for the buyers, from the marketing side of things.

Like Going to the Store

The positioning analogy I use is the grocery store. The grocery store positions the most expensive products at eye level, unless they are nutritionally poor. In that case, they put them at the kids` level of their shelving units. They offer other products at other values, but they increase the chances of you buying the most expensive items and your children selecting the unhealthy choices, by proper positioning. **When a product is not selling, they reposition it.**

Mastering communications

In Real Estate, using suitable language can make sellers feel much more comfortable. The competition or "active listings" become "unsold property." It is not active, but unsold, which sounds much less challenging. Your fair market value now becomes your competitive positioning, because you can never speak of true value, unless somebody has paid it. The listing price will become your initial market positioning and price reductions now become "repositions." Instead of saying, we will now have to reduce the price, you will say, "We are going to reposition your home," which sounds much less negative, no doubt.

Avoid using the term "dropping prices" because sellers get tired of hearing the term "price reductions." Instead talk about repositioning. For example the "buyer pool is not responding to your current price position. So, we need to reposition your home, Mr. and Mrs. Seller." Delete the word "comparable" from your vocabulary. Honestly, there are not any houses that are similar or equal to the sellers`, just ask them. There is not one house that compares to theirs or is similar to it.

Thinking like a Buyer

Here is a dialog that I would encourage you to use; "Mr. and Mrs. Seller, we need to position your home, so that it will pop-out in this market. It needs to be **in the market and not on the market.**" You need to make them understand the difference. Another tip has to do with their mindset: "If you want to catch a buyer, Mr. and Mrs. Seller, then we need to think like a buyer. Would a buyer look at everything? Will they look at a limited number of other houses? Would there be other sub-areas that they might consider? Would there be other communities they might consider? How far will a buyer go to expand their search until they narrow it down to what they are looking for?" Once your sellers understand how buyers think, they will be much more relaxed and cooperative.

When you are positioning property, don't think and present your plans to your sellers as if they were small. Think BIG. For example, study and present the buyer demographics of the property you are selling. Is it a baby boomer, a retired person, a double income person, a first time home buyer, or a young family? Take the time to explore that with your sellers and understand the demographics of your possible buyers.

Visual aids

The Full-list technique

A visual pricing technique I like to use with sellers is what I call the **full-list technique.** When meeting with the sellers, bring a long print-out list of all the unsold property in a large search parameter, say, within a ten mile-radius of their home. Then, bring a short list of sold property; a list of the people who were successful in the course of the last sixty days. Hold the two lists up beside each other and see what your sellers` response will be. This visual aid will help your seller understand the job you have ahead of you.

Before you first visit the sellers' home, here is a line I recommend you use, in order to facilitate a full listing: "Mr. and Mrs. Seller, I would like to do some research on your home before I meet with you. Can you give me a position or price point I could research for you?"

The Shopping Cart Analogy

I also use another great visual technique. I call it the "shopping cart" visual. Just like grocery store shoppers, we all tend to look for the shortest lines and the carts with the smallest loads. In Real Estate, we can't choose the line that we want to be in. In my little technique, the unsold property represents the number of people in the checkout line. The list of property that has sold represents the sellers that have already checked out successfully this month. After showing them the two lists, you ask your clients, "how important is it to you to move through this line in 30, 60, 90 days? In this particular position, your home would be here and this is how long it would take for you to successfully check out of the grocery store line."

Ask your sellers where they want to be in this line. It is their choice how they want to position their property. They now know how many people are getting through the line in a month and how many have checked out (sold).

You will be using the term initial market position for listing price and the term repositioning for a price reduction. You need to reposition the sellers' home whenever buyer pools are not responding to sellers' expectations.

Once you master these techniques, you will go from "catching" to "fishing" for buyers; and that is really where you want to be.

Here are some lines that I have frequently used:

USEFUL DIALOG LINES

"Mr. and Mrs. Seller, I just attended an advanced seminar on market research. I ran a market study of your home and found some great information that will help us better understand what is happening in today's market. Can we get together and go over this information? Would you like me to share with you the power of repositioning your property in this particular market?"

"I am so sorry, Mr. and Mrs. Seller. You seem to want to determine how much you want for your home. This is not how it works, unfortunately. Do you want your home to be on the market, or do you want your home to be in the market, because there is a difference."

"NAR reports that you are in the market when one in ten physical showings generates an offer, and 100 online visitors should generate one physical showing. Have you had ten physical showings? Then you should have had an offer, maybe not an accepted offer but at least an offer. If you haven't, then your home is not properly positioned."

"Mr. and Mrs. Seller, for every 100 online visitors we should have generated one physical showing in the market. If you have had between 2 and 300 online viewings and no physical showing, your property is not positioned properly according to NAR statistics. Mr. and Mrs. Seller, we can either try to meet the marketplace or wait for the market to change. In today's market, you must move and change your bait."

10

Features vs. benefits

"Features tell, benefits sell"

Marketing 101

One of the areas in Real Estate I find agents often misunderstand is the power of **benefit selling as opposed to feature selling**. In sales, the customer buys the benefit, not the feature. For example, we don't buy a house because it has central air-conditioning. We buy a house because of the benefits of having air conditioning in the summer. We enjoy that feeling of having a cool temperature inside the house. It is the benefit of that projected feeling which stimulates us to buy.

For example, imagine you are buying a power drill from a salesperson who explains all the features of the drill, including power, speed, and the quality of the drill bit. Let me ask you this question, why do we want to buy a power drill? I would imagine it is because we need to poke a hole somewhere. You want to focus on the fact that **the benefit of that power drill is the hole**. You don't need to emphasize the features of the power drill or the drill bit, you must stress the drill's ability to produce a quick, clean, hassle-free hole every time. The salesman in the example is busy selling the features; while he is forgetting what his customer is really after; namely, the benefits.

Selling the hole, and not the drill

There are many areas in Real Estate where the features are over-emphasized. For example, providing a market assessment on someone's property is the feature. The benefit is that, by using that assessment, the sellers know exactly what they can expect to get for their property; with no surprises. They will know exactly where their financial position is, in case they want to reinvest, and they will know what they can expect to get for their property and what kind of net profit they might end up with in their pockets. Those are the benefits that you need to emphasize on, rather than the market assessment itself.

Making listings competitive

Offering tips and information to help sellers make their property more salable is a feature that many agents use, to attract potential sellers. Very few agents emphasize on the benefits to sellers of providing a service that will make their home more competitive, or help it sell for more money or faster, with little or no inconvenience. These benefits are what sellers are looking for.

Managing Timing

Advice on timing is a great feature that you are offering prospective buyers and sellers. The benefit you must emphasize is that timing in Real Estate is everything. Knowing a year's breakdown, in terms of the best selling and buying times, and the actual length of time the process takes, is crucial. It is not the feature of timing that is attractive, but the benefit of knowing when are the best moments to buy for less or sell for more money.

Financing Tips

Another feature you are offering is advice on financing. The benefits you need to emphasize for clients are: learning what they can actually afford, how to get set up with the best interest rate, and how to use a mortgage broker versus a lending institution, which will save them time and money.

Renovation Advice

Estimating property repairs is another feature you may offer. In this case, the associated benefits will be that clients will learn that, for every dollar they put in, they are going to get five dollars back. You will inform them about the best vendors and contractors, so that they can get the biggest returns on their renovation investment, saving them time, money, and disappointment.

The self-sale

Giving tips to people on selling their home themselves is also a feature. What are the benefits of this? Well, when you are doing this, you emphasize the prospects' ability to do it themselves, saving time and money. You guide them towards learning how to qualify, how to get better results, how to ensure that they have a secure and binding contract. You must engage your customer with the benefits, not the features.

Advertising Assistance

When it comes to offering advice on advertising, I see many agents offering advertising tips. This is only the feature. The benefits will be that clients will know where buyers are coming from, they will understand which kinds of advertising work and which don't, thus saving time and money. These are all great benefits that will encourage potential sellers to work with you.

Market tips

Sharing information about the competition in the area is another important feature in your package to attract sellers. The benefits are that clients will learn how to keep their property's pricing competitive. Knowing the competition gives clients an edge. It helps them make sure that their house will sell before others do.

Measuring Success, Assessing Failure

A final example of a feature commonly used as a sales point in Real Estate is offering advice on why a prospect's house didn't sell. The benefit of this feature is that clients can identify the mistakes they made and avoid making them again. This will enable them to be prepared to get their home sold the second time around, instead of having it just sit in the market. These are all great benefits that will encourage expired listing sellers to contact you.

Benefit selling versus feature selling is one of the areas where you can make a fundamental switch in the way you are doing business, with the most dramatic results. This exercise will also help you capture and engage people, instead of sounding just like every other agent in the business.

Psychology in Sales

Getting inside their head

How successful do you think you could be in Real Estate, if you could understand what the prospects were thinking before you even met them? Understanding your prospect's mindset is a powerful skill that you should take the time to learn and master.

These are the things on your prospects` minds before they meet you. Now, what is your mindset? In order to become a top producer in Real Estate, your mindset needs to start with confidence. Top agents don't meet with sellers hoping to get their listing. Top agents believe they have a choice of who they want to work with. Top agents meet with sellers to see if they even want their listing and to see if the prospects are their ideal type of customer.

Top agents are masters of rapport building and taking the time to sell themselves to their clients, before they try to sell them on anything else. We have all heard the famous Zig Ziglar quote **"People don't care how much you know until they know how much you care about them."** Focus on the clients and build some rapport and trust. A simple and powerful way of doing this is to ask clients questions about themselves. Be an active listener and write their responses down. Always be aware and focus your mindset on relationships first and business second.

5 ELEMENTS OF PROSPECT MINDSETS

1. They're thinking that **there is no way they are going to sign anything**. They tend to be on the defensive.

2. They feel **they have to like you first**, making sure that you are a professional, before they consider doing business with you.

3. **They don't know what it is they don't know** about Real Estate dealings. You must help them discover what *they don't know*, so they will appreciate what *you* know.

4. **They are unsure whether your presence is helping** them or not. You must make them feel glad that you came.

5. **They need to feel comfortable around you and trust you**. The fastest way to achieve this is to show them that you care, asking them questions about themselves. Use the FORD method to build trust quickly, which is the most valuable skill in sales.

Now, what is on your mind?

Top producers' mindset also involves a readiness for problem solving. Most clients are going to have a people problem, a price problem or a situation problem. You must be aware of this and listen to their issues. It is your job to help them discover exactly what their problems are and offer them solutions to resolve them. After discovering their problems, you can say to them, "something you said earlier concerns me, but here is how I think we can handle it, and here are some of the solutions that we might be able to implement."

Making decisions happen

Last, but not least, you are going to help clients make a definite decision. You are going to get a flat-out "yes" or "no," and not a "maybe" or an "I will think about it." Top producers have a mind to look for a decision. They are out to get either a clear "no" or a signature/firm decision. They have a gut feeling that makes them stick around until a definite decision has been made. Learn to wait until you get what you came for. What do you have to lose? Think about how much time you have already invested on evaluations, analyses, and meetings.

Top performers will say "You need to think about it? Not a problem. I will now go out to my car and return some phone calls. So, take all the time you need to discuss it." Another option is to get a **post-dated listing contract** and say "Take the time to think about it. I understand it is a big decision, and I don't want to pressure you into anything. Why don't I just post-date the contract? I still have the signature, and I will give you a courtesy call and make sure that we activate it knowing that it has been approved." If they just want to have that time, that's fine. Give them the time to think, but get the signature, and leave with the signature and a decision, one way or another.

Top Producers would rather know when the client feels that they are not the agent they want to do business with. When this happens, thank them for being honest. Top producers would rather hear a far more discouraging truth than an "I'll think about it" or an "I will call you." Always wish the clients well and let them know that, if the opportunity to do business arises, you would be pleased to seize that opportunity. Then you can either keep in touch with them, or just move on to the next client.

11

Getting in a rut, and how to get out of it

In different moments in your life, you will find yourself getting into a rut or a sales slump. All salespeople want to know what to do to kick-start their business and get out of that kind of rut. Here is my take on it.

22 solutions to Kick-Start your Business (and yourself!)

1. Start extending all of your listings for another 60-90 days and, while you are at it, get a price reduction.

2. Prepare new evaluations and new assessments on all of your current listings. Include the latest and current statistics, because it may have been weeks or months since you made your initial assessment of the property.

3. Use new photography, maybe hire a professional to take interior photos and get fresh material in place.

4. Prepare a price reduction flyer and postcard.

5. Go around your listings' neighborhoods delivering just-listed and just-sold cards, price reduction cards or open house postcards. Introduce yourself and canvas the area to find prospects, perhaps friends or family of the people living in the neighbourhood, who might be interested in moving there.

6. Send a letter to your past and present clients asking for feedback. Give them a survey to find out what you could be doing better.

7. Identify 100 of your last buyers and put them in a follow-up system. Update and purge your existing database, upgrade new addresses, collect birthdays or anniversaries. Spend some time talking to some of your clients, because it might be time to purge some of them from your database.

8. Approach an expired listing, using the tactics described earlier.

9. Clean up your desk, office, briefcase, and vehicle. Do something new and different that gives you a fresh start and re-energizes you.

10. Reset and re-establish goals. Look at the next 90 days and re-evaluate your personal, family, financial, business, and spiritual to-do-list. Get a new family photo or a new business photo.

11. Prospect every day. Get back to basics. Look at all of the different methods of prospecting. Identify the ones you used to make money at and start doing them again.

12. Call your past customers and thank them for being a part of your success.

13. Get a haircut, start exercising, and evaluate your health.

14. Pick up a classic and read a good book such as Napoleon Hill's *"Think and Grow Rich,"* or George Clason's *"The Richest Man in Babylon,"* or Dale Carnegie's *"How to Win Friends and Influence People."*

15. Review your personal and business budgets.

16. Treat your spouse, or a friend/family member to a special day

17. Get up one hour earlier for a week and see what happens.

18. Clean up a mess or a problematic personal situation.

19. Arrange a special birthday party, anniversary or holiday for your family, or plan a special event for you and your spouse.

20. Call someone you know and have not talked to for some time. Ask them if they know of a friend who might be interested in talking to somebody about buying or selling Real Estate.

21. Attend a class or conference, and consider hiring a coach or mentor.

22. Arrange breakfast or lunch with a group of successful people and compare notes and ideas.

Not only are these great ways to kick-start your business, but I also recommend doing them once every four months to keep you and your business on track.

12

The difference between taking a listing and taking a salable listing

It is important to know and understand that there is a big difference between taking a listing and taking a salable listing. The list below is meant to help you understand that difference, so you can put that knowledge to work for you and your business.

Six truths about taking a salable listing

1. You are in an inventory business, where listings are the name of the game. You have to get the listings to get their profitable spin-offs as well. Just because you can sell, it doesn't mean that you can list. Develop your listing presentations. Knowing the power of inventory and how to get spin-offs from it is the key.

2. Don't waste your time on prospects who don't seem motivated. They will cost you time and money and probably contribute to ruining your reputation. When the market is challenging, what message are you giving if your listing doesn't sell? It is better not to have listings than to have listings that don't sell. Don't take a listing for the sake of taking a listing. You will know when to do it, if you evaluate the seller's motivation.

3. Advertising is not going to sell an unsalable listing. Taking on a full page ad is futile, if the property is not priced properly. Your ad will not change the market, so stop investing in that kind of advertising, and understand that the listing needs to be either repositioned or removed.

4. No amount of servicing will sell an unsalable listing. World-class service and open houses won't sell it. Reduce the price of the home, if there is no interest. The market is sometimes unkind, but it never lies when it comes to pricing. No amount of advertising or servicing is going to sell a house that is not in a position to be sold.

5. There can be nothing wrong with property that price cannot cure. If a house is on a high traffic street, cosmetically challenged by this location, just reduce the price. You don't need to spend thousands in advertising or remodeling. You can change the price or reposition the home, and it will sell. I always say to people who want more money that they have two options. The first one is to drop the price and the second option is to drop the house onto a flat-bed truck and move it into a neighborhood where it will be worth more money. Wouldn't it be easier to just drop the price?

   Take Wal-Mart for example. If something is not selling on their shelves, they don't advertise it more, they don't move it around, and they don't spend more time on it. They just slash the price and move on. If Canadian Tire isn't selling tires, they drop the tire prices. It is not that difficult to understand that price will cure anything.

6. We are not magicians in Real Estate. Educate the sellers about the fact that the heavy duty nails, the geothermal heating, and the teak shelves in the garage don't mean a thing to a prospective buyer. These things don't make a home more expensive, they just make it more competitive. Don't tell the owners that you will sell a house for a price that the property is not really worth. Stop promising something that won't happen and just say no.

Price and Prejudice

There are three things to consider when pricing property. You must establish the right price, the right terms, and the right time duration. What do I mean by the right terms? These could be an assumable mortgage[9], vendor take-back incentives, commissions, trades, and other similar benefits.

Imagine you are considering taking a 1-year listing. Is there a right price, right terms or a right duration? If you get one of these three things, then take the listing. If you can't get a single one of them, just walk away.

According to an official Canadian study:

CHANCES OF SELLING A HOME

95% if it is within the market's value range

50% if listed **5% above** market value

35% if listed **10% above** market value

25% if listed **15% above** market value

That is only a one-in-four chance of selling for a price 15% above market value!

---

[9] A financing arrangement where the outstanding mortgage is transferred from owner to buyer The buyer assumes the owner's debts, and is saved the complication of obtaining their own mortgage.

Making listings more salable

Insider's Tips

Here are some tips for helping a listing become more salable. This is a great tool to use with sellers, to give the chances of them selling their property a dramatic boost.

1. **Proper pricing**: offering the best bang for your buck and having it priced properly is the key to successfully making a listing more salable.

2. **If you can't get them to list at the sharpest price, then try offering an incentive** like vendor financing, an assumable mortgage, or a small take-back mortgage[10].

3. **Offer cash back incentives or deals** where the seller carries ten percent down, or offer below market down-payments and low interest rates. Offer to buy down[11] the buyer's interest rates through a mortgage broker.

4. **Put up post-dated price reductions.** When I take a listing, I always take post-dated price reductions at the initial listing. It is a lot easier to phone sellers with the courtesy call and let them know that their price has been reduced every two to three weeks, rather than to have to go over there and fight with the seller to try and get them to reduce their price.

5. **Use an odd sale price** like $288,888 or $495,123 Odd sale prices stand out more than the even, the 900's or the .99 price points which are normally used.

6. **Add six months or one year of listing time** to listing agreements. With enough time, the market may catch up or the seller may become more motivated.

---

[10] A type of mortgage where sellers offer to lend funds to buyers, in order to facilitate the sale

[11] A buy down involves the buyer or seller offering a lump sum payment that will reduce the mortgage's interest rates.

7. **Offer above-market incentive commissions** for the selling realtor. Offer cash bonuses or furniture package bonuses to prospective buyers, if they buy within a certain period of time.

8. **Give easy access.** Quick easy access to property entices people for quick showings. Nothing is worse than having to drive across town to pick up keys or waiting to show a listing to an anxious buyer.

9. **Use larger SIGNS. 60% of all initial property calls come from signage.** Have a larger sign, multiple signs, or better positioned signs.

10. **Offer and advise prospective buyers that immediate possession is available.** They want to know that they can get into their new home in 2 weeks or 2 months, and this could be the difference between them buying your listing or not.

11. **Offer trading options**, for example trading up or trading down, or offering a boat, a trailer or something of the like as a trade incentive.

12. **Offer extras** like vacations, appliances, furniture, entertainment systems, hot tubs, and even vehicles to prospective buyers.

13. **Have an independent certified appraisal done.**

14. **Have the property properly surveyed** and provide legal surveys and title insurance to prospective buyers.

15. **Have a pre-listing property inspection done** and take care of all the deficiencies on the report prior to marketing the home.

16. **Avoid "subject to the sale of" clauses.** You don't want to take a listing, unless you know that the other listing is salable. There is nothing worse than losing business by being unable to sell tied-up property.

17. **Offering office caravan tours**[12] or private agent luncheons, may aid in making listings more salable.

18. **Complete obvious repairs, get the home staged and properly set up for showing.** Hire someone to come in and do a makeover on the yard or the whole house, with a new paint job.

19. **Provide the seller with a list of all of these ideas** and put the monkey on their back, instead of having it look like it is your fault that the house isn't more salable and competitive. Let them know that they need to follow your advice, if they want the sale to happen.

These ideas will help you get peoples' property *in* **the market** and not just **on the market.**

However big a **recession** the country may be going through, **whether other agents are not doing very well,** or houses are **becoming tougher to sell.**

These simple tips and guidelines will help you **stay ahead of the game.**

If you believe in yourself and play your cards right, you will never have to worry. Times when other people would worry will become times to get out there and get RESULTS. The wide array of proven strategies contained in this material will hopefully change your business and your life. They surely changed mine.

---

12 This is where a group of different agents visit several listings in a particular area. Their input and different perspectives can give you a fresh approach on selling a home.

Conclusion

"In my experience, in the real-estate business ... We must continually reinvent ourselves, responding to changing times with innovative new business models."

Akira Mori

Throughout these pages, you have been treading the paths of success in the Real Estate business, in the light of my personal experience as a successful Realtor. From the big picture, which is all about improving yourself, working hard on finding prospects, and really connecting with people, you need to go into the details of what needs to be done every day. I hope that this book will help you define your business and personal goals. I wish for it to motivate you into going that extra mile, so that you can reap the profits later.

Chapter summary

In the very first chapter, you learned about the importance of "Crunching the numbers" of your business. You have to make a soul-searching and honest effort as to your present standing in the Real Estate business. This includes your official and personal expenses, your break-even point to stay in the business and the listings and closings you need to make in order to meet your expenses and make a profit on top.

In the second chapter, we discussed prospecting skills; communication with your customers and developing and sustaining relationships, to take your business from the size it is today to a future of sustained growth.

In the third chapter, we focused on prospecting methods and tips for running Open Houses, including practical tips and tricks, as well as lines of dialogue that may come in handy in these situations.

Chapters four and five dealt with Prospecting Methods; Farming, Direct Mail, and Cold Calling. Each section offered detailed advice on how to go about each one of these methods, in order to maximize your time and effort.

Chapter six focused on those opportunities that lie right in front of you, but which are not recognized by you, such as making use of Expired Listings and helping For-Sale-By-Owner prospects sell their property themselves. Most Real Estate Agents are never aware of these opportunities, and making use of them will give you an invaluable competitive advantage.

Chapter seven highlights a very important factor in everybody's life: Time Management. If you learn the techniques I put forth in this chapter as to how you can make the best use of the same 24 hours that all of us have each day, this will help you achieve success in both your business and your personal life.

In Chapter eight, I tried to stress the importance of having the right mental attitude as a Real Estate businessman, by analyzing methods for "going from good to great". If you diligently follow these methods and pay heed to the advice provided in this chapter, you are sure to take your business from good to great.

The Pricing Strategies elaborately discussed in chapter 9 include all the tricks of the trade, as practiced by a successful Realtor. Here is a final tip on the subject: never mention the words "price" or "comparable" to sellers when referring to their property.

By now, I am sure you can clearly understand the difference between feature selling and benefit selling described in chapter 10. Thus, you can properly explain to your prospects a whole set of benefits which derive from a house's/deal's features.

Know the power of the two important words "You" and "Why" in sales and selling, as described in chapter 11. When using these words frequently in your business, you will prosper.

Chapter 12 tells you how to effectively manage your business, taking it out of a rough spot, and into success.

The difference between "taking a listing and taking a salable listing" as explained in Chapter 13 will save you from carrying deadweights in your business. Follow these techniques and half your headaches will cease to exist.

Finally, you are offered purposeful, practical, and simple tips to make a listing more salable on Chapter 14.

Read this book with concentration, repeatedly if needed. Mark the points you consider the most useful for you and refer to them whenever you are in doubt. By following this simple advice, you will, in time, see yourself being transformed into a Successful Realtor.

7-figure income, me?

If you have paid close attention to the contents of this material, you know that I am not trying to give you a magic overnight formula to become a millionaire, like the ones that abound today. This is a full program. It is based on a realistic assessment of what is going on in the market today.[13]

---

[13]　There is much more in store for you to aid your success. This e-book shall be followed by webinars, a DVD, and a CD Rom with training materials and tools for Real Estate success. You are definitely in for Success in your Real Estate business.

If you want to take your Real Estate business to the top, you can do it; but there will be a lot of work involved. More than work, (you are probably working harder now for much smaller results) you will need to change EVERYTHING about the way you do business. The change involves a complete switch of mind maps and assumptions about Real Estate and the challenges our profession involves.

However, because this is not a magic recipe, trust me on this; do it well enough and it might just...work!

Start *doing things differently* TODAY and success will be yours. It is all about the *doing*. I wish you the best for the rest of your brilliant Real Estate career.

Wade Webb

Made in the USA
Columbia, SC
05 March 2021